# Praise for *Other A...*

"In this book, Shanta Nimba... recounting how cooperation crea... ...and
consumers by developing a food system that not only promoted
healthy food but wove within it practices that respect workers and
the environment."
 —E. Kim Coontz, executive director, California Center for
 Cooperative Development

"Anyone who cares about progressive social change should ponder
the history of the Bay Area food co-op movement of the 1970s."
 —John Curl, author of *For All the People: Uncovering the
 Hidden History of Cooperation, Cooperative Movements, and
 Communalism in America*

"I have been waiting more than twenty years for this book! Shanta
Nimbark Sacharoff's *Other Avenues Are Possible* details the history of the People's Food System, a grand experiment in combining good food and workplace democracy. *Other Avenues* answers
many of my questions about how the food politics of the Bay Area
developed and points the way towards a better—and more cooperative—future. A must-read for anyone who eats food."
 —Gordon Edgar, author of *Cheesemonger: A Life on the Wedge*
 and a worker owner of Rainbow Grocery Cooperative

"Shanta Sacharoff has written an illuminating account of the power and potential of food cooperatives. *Other Avenues Are Possible*
sheds light on the many possibilities and challenges of community
and individual participation in the way we acquire and share our
food. This book is about building a healthier world, engaging communities, and driving social and civic responsibility. In order to
understand the eddying forces that constrain and control the food
that we put on our plate, read this fascinating book."
 —Jaya Padmanabhan, editor of *India Currents*

# Other Avenues Are Possible
## Legacy of the People's Food System
## of the San Francisco Bay Area

## Shanta Nimbark Sacharoff

*Other Avenues Are Possible: Legacy of the People's Food System of the San Francisco Bay Area*
Shanta Nimbark Sacharoff
This edition copyright ©2016 PM Press
© Shanta Nimbark Sacharoff

ISBN: 978-1-62963-232-2
Library of Congress Control Number: 2016948142

Cover by John Yates/Stealworks.com
Interior by Jonathan Rowland

10 9 8 7 6 5 4 3 2 1

PM Press
PO Box 23912
Oakland, CA 94623
www.pmpress.org

Printed in the USA by the Employee Owners of Thomson-Shore in Dexter, Michigan.
www.thomsonshore.com

# Contents

# PREFACE

SOME YEARS AGO, my young neighbor, who was in second grade, asked me for help with his homework assignment. "I have to do a five-minute interview to learn survey skills. Can I interview you?" He had three questions:

> Question #1: "Do you work?"
> My answer: "Yes."
> Question #2: "Where do you work?"
> My answer: "At a food co-op."
> Question #3: "Do you like your work?"
> My answer: "I love it!"

The boy was so excited he almost fell off the chair. I asked why he was so happy, and he replied that out of the six people he interviewed, I was the only one who loved my job—and that made his day. Others had said that they worked for money or to keep busy or because it was the thing to do, but mine was the only affirmative response to work that he received. Many years later, I still feel the same way. I love my workplace and the community it supports, and I feel that my work contributes something positive to the world.

This book tells the story of the food co-ops and the complex of community businesses that thrived in the San Francisco Bay Area during the late 1960s and '70s. The system was built by a group of people dedicated to harnessing the power of collaborative community to obtain and share healthy food or "Food for People, Not for Profit." My personal journey within this movement included working in many capacities as a cooperator and also creating and then sharing recipes with others. While participating in this movement I came to understand the powerful positive effects that our work can have on our community.

This is the story of the many people who came together to bring healthy food to the people, building a strong foundation for the co-operative business models of today. Their experience bears witness to the ways that the workplace can change, replacing hierarchical models with participatory democracy.

The global economy is unstable, with an increasing gap between the haves and have-nots. World food security is under constant threat. Now more than ever, we need guidance to bring back sanity and a vision of sustainability for the future. The People's Food System was a humble experiment by the food-system visionaries of the San Francisco Bay Area, with the participation of thousands of people. Their experience left us a platform from which to address vital questions, such as how can concerned citizens work toward global food sovereignty and create a more equitable distribution of food in today's economy? This book offers information and resources to help create new co-ops and build enthusiasm for future generations to continue this work. Today's co-ops can offer direction for harnessing the power of collaborative community and hope for the future.

# INTRODUCTION

FOOD, WONDERFUL FOOD!! In ancient Sanskrit writings food is compared to Brahma himself, the Creator, Giver of Life. Food not only sustains our bodies, but also unites the spirit of the people who share it. The way that a society grows and distributes its food says a lot about the strength and resourcefulness of its communities. Food gathering, distribution, preparation, and sharing all offer natural opportunities for connection to the larger world. On every level, food connects humans in social interaction, community collaboration, and political development.

Not long ago, farming was a shared experience between growers and consumers, and in many agrarian societies it continues to be so today. Since the industrial revolution, much of the world's farmland has become a commodity owned by agro-capitalists motivated purely by gain, who systematically destroy fragile ecosystems, diluting our food with fillers and preservatives, and packaging it for maximum profit.

When I first came to New York from a small Indian village, I was astounded to read the label on a can of peas and find that it contained as many as twelve ingredients, only one of which was the peas. Later, when I moved to San Francisco in the mid-1970s, I was delighted to find many small shops selling bulk food out of burlap sacks the way they do in India. Corporate food chains such as Whole Foods and Trader Joe's had not yet arrived in the Bay Area. Instead, there was a small group of Real Food Company stores, a number of health food corner stores, ethnic markets, and farmers markets offering alternatives to the packaged foods sold by the big grocery stores. Going to the Alemany Farmers Market for the first time and seeing all the colorful seasonal produce sold by farmers was truly an ecstatic experience for me! And there, I met people of many ethnicities from various parts of the world willing to share and exchange recipes and cooking techniques.

Soon I discovered the San Francisco Food Conspiracy, a group of people who had organized to buy fresh and bulk food together and to share progressive ideas of a sustainable lifestyle with like-minded folks. In the 1970s, everything was conspiratorial and exciting, and I joined the club; it shaped my food choices and my work forever.

As Food Conspiracy members, we ordered, divided, and often cooked and ate our food together. We educated one another about the politics of food and rallied together against the corporate takeover of our food sources and distribution systems.

When the Food Conspiracy became too large to manage from houses and garages, we began to open storefront outlets. I started to volunteer at one of the first stores to open, the Haight Community Food Store, and embarked upon a lifetime commitment to the Bay Area's food co-ops. I began to participate in a dynamic movement that shaped the small experimental food-sharing clubs into a significant number of democratic workplaces. Later, I became a worker-owner of Other Avenues Food Store Cooperative. Working there for more than three decades, I witnessed the growth, changes, and challenges of the Bay Area's food co-ops.

This book tells the story of a community's shared dream of a food distribution system where farmers, wholesalers, delivery people, worker-owners, and shoppers all cooperated to support a vision of sustainable farming and a clean planet through their work options and food choices. It is the story of a community that created viable tools for sustainability by believing that other avenues are possible!

# PART I
# COOPERATION BUILDS
# COMMUNITY

COOPERATION IS CENTRAL to human evolution. Early civilization took a major leap forward when people began to realize the power of collaboration to build communities. Just as the invention of the wheel enabled a new level of mechanical efficiency, so a circle of people contributing their many hands to making unwieldy tasks easier allowed communities to prosper. Even more, working together and sharing experiences brought a new and greater level of kinship.

The first evidence of organized cooperative activities is associated with our modern human ancestor, *Homo erectus*, who lived in communities 1.5 million years ago in Africa.[1] As early nomadic peoples organized for common welfare, they cooperated to meet their basic needs for food and shelter. Elaborate rituals and taboos evolved to reinforce values and social norms favoring cooperation, in order to hold these constantly challenged societies together.

## Early Cooperatives

As human societies transitioned from nomadic to agrarian, people gathered into groups seasonally to engage in common activities, including planting and harvesting food. These food-related activities proved advantageous, and cooperative ventures spread into other areas. As a result, the first social codes of cooperation developed, redefining family and other immediate social groups. As people settled and formed principalities, they developed formal rules for cooperation: essentially an early form of society. When the stratification of resources and power began to play a role in early administration, cooperative groups either weakened or grew stronger, depending on their ability to respond. Over time, models of cooperation were codified and handed down through the generations as norms of social behavior, eventually becoming incorporated into systems of tribal law, community regulations, and subtle social rules.

The development of formalized cooperative rules is often credited to Europeans, but records from older civilizations, China and Babylonia among them, clearly indicate the existence of organized cooperation. Some of these cultures had public codes permitting people to form cooperatives to procure food for all. In ancient Babylonia, King Hammurabi's (2067–2025 BC) famous codes specifically allowed farmers to manage the "largest estates on a cooperative basis . . . where tenants kept strict account of their enterprises."[2] In this way, poor farmers achieved a level of economic freedom.

Most traditional history books evaluate the strength of ancient civilizations, including Egypt, Greece, and Rome, by measuring the military triumphs of powerful heroes and their empires, but this ignores the role of cooperation among the common people. In spite of strong archeological evidence of the high levels of cooperation necessary among workers to achieve monumental tasks, such as building the pyramids, these stories go untold. Fleets of ships built for war; volumes of food grown, harvested, and stored; herds of animals gathered and tended; the building of homes; and the manufacture of housewares, textiles, and ceramics—these were often cooperative ventures.

Many historical accounts indicate that workers and the elite often shared food at celebrations and public events, festivals, and feasts. Food sharing not only united people of similar backgrounds, it reinforced the strong bonds that permeated all levels of society.

## Notes

1. Kimberly A. Zeuli and Robert Cropp, *Cooperatives: Principles and Practices in the 21st Century* (Madison: University of Wisconsin, Center of Cooperatives, 2007), 1.
2. Ewell Paul Roy, *Cooperatives: Development, Principles, and Management*, 3rd edition (Danville, IL: Interstate Printers and Publishers Inc., 1976), 41–42.

# CHAPTER 1
# FOOD COOPERATIVES IN
# THE UNITED STATES

EARLY EUROPEANS WHO came to settle in the United States were surprised to observe Native Americans working together. According to some historical observations, "ownership in our sense did not exist."[1]

> "Planting, cultivating, and harvesting of crops were highly organized cooperative activities, cooperation in this instance being stimulated by the desire to enjoy the pleasure of group work."[2]

The ability of Native American tribes to cooperatively produce and trade goods is well documented in the writing of Columbus who sailed to the Americas from Europe.

> "The Indians," Columbus reported, "are so naïve and so free with their possessions that no one who has not witnessed them would believe it. When you ask for something they have, they never say no. To the contrary, they offer to share with anyone."[3]

In addition to sharing lifesaving local food gifts, such as pumpkin, corn, beans, and turkey, as well as medicinal plants, with Europeans, Native Americans also taught the settlers valuable lessons about cooperative farming and trading. The constitutional ideas of Franklin and Jefferson were profoundly influenced by their observations of the egalitarian forms of governance among Native Americans.[4]

Collaboration was instrumental to group survival in colonial America, and intentional cooperatives grew up among the European settlers. Shared labor was a common practice, from harvesting crops to quilting. Cooperative acts among the settlers saved many lives during disasters. Mutual Aid Societies were formed to share resources and to maintain the identities of groups from various countries. Spontaneous gatherings to prepare and consume food were common. Feasts like the one commemorated by the Thanksgiving holiday occurred regularly and served to strengthen the connections among colonists of varying backgrounds.

## Co-ops and the Industrial Revolution

During the Industrial Revolution, there was a strong wave of organized cooperatives for a different reason: working people united to combat the increasing exploitative nature of industrial corporate power. Active resistance by workers against unfair labor practices was instrumental in stimulating the formation of the first organized labor cooperatives in the United States.

Optimistic thinkers had predicted that machines would free the working class. Instead, as new technologies made the workforce more productive, opportunistic businesses began to exploit their workers by increasing work hours at the lowest possible wages. Factory workers and farmers united in defiance. In the early 1800s, industrial workers reacted by marching, striking, and boycotting to demand better working conditions and reasonable wages. Small groups of striking workers typically joined together to address hardship and share their reduced food resources. The first formal modern food cooperatives were born of this socioeconomic upheaval.

In 1844, a group of weavers in Rochdale, England responded to harsh working conditions and low wages by opening a store where they purchased and shared food cooperatively. Later, they opened storefront outlets and agreed upon some rules, known as the Rochdale Cooperative Principles. These principles helped members and co-ops organize democratically to meet their shared needs. Inspired by the success of the Rochdale Cooperative, other cooperative ventures arose in England and the United States. The Rochdale weavers have been credited with initiating modern cooperatives in Europe.

In 1895, the International Co-operative Alliance (ICA) was formed, uniting co-ops from many countries. The ICA defined a cooperative as "an autonomous association of persons united voluntarily to meet their common economic and cultural needs and aspirations through a jointly-owned and democratically controlled enterprise."[5] In 2013, the ICA had 272 members in ninety-four countries.

> *The Rochdale Cooperative Principles as revised and adopted by the International Alliance of Cooperatives (ICA) in 1995.*[6]
>
> (1) **Voluntary, Open Membership** to all without gender, social, racial, political, or religious discrimination
> (2) **Democratic Member Control** based on equal rights of members; one member, one vote
> (3) **Member Economic Participation** by contributing capital equitably and dividing surplus among members in proportion to their transactions within the co-op
> (4) **Autonomy and Independence of Cooperatives** through self-help and control by members
> (5) **Education of Cooperative Principles and Information** to members and the public
> (6) **Cooperation among Cooperatives** on local, national, and international levels
> (7) **Concern for the Community and Its Development** through policies accepted by the members

In the United States, Europeans and other early American immigrants had started to organize cooperatives with formalized principles even before the Rochdale Cooperative was created. When money and other tangible resources were scarce, cooperative commerce was the only solution. In 1785, a group of American farmers organized to create the Philadelphia Society for Promotion of Agriculture.[7] Influenced later by the Rochdale model, other types of co-ops formed, including the Boston Mechanics' and Laborers' Mutual Benefit Association, in 1845. Although cooperatives opened in other economic sectors, food-related businesses were among the first groups to formalize as cooperatives in the United States.

At the other end of the spectrum, by the mid-1800s growing numbers of agricultural corporations were changing food from a basic human need to a business commodity. The government's economic policies increasingly favored wealthy speculators who gambled on farm "futures," using food to balance international trade. Business interests demanded that farmers produce more food, regulating the industry so that individual farmers had less control over the means of production. When industrial development began to threaten farmers' autonomy, American farmers began to form cooperatives as a platform to reassert control over food production. They organized marketing co-ops to counter the adverse effects of overproduction and price controls that kept prices of farm products artificially low. Farmers, farmworkers, and consumers all came to understand that they would be more secure acting cooperatively than they could be acting separately. The Farmers' Alliance, founded in 1875 in the American South, and the American Society of Equity, formed in 1902, were both strong examples of early cooperatives that emerged in response to economic upheaval in the United States.[8] These and other co-ops like them became the basis for a larger agricultural cooperative movement.

At the same time, a different wave of cooperatives was taking form among the many people who had migrated from rural areas to industrial towns looking for work. Having to rely upon urban markets for their food, these people had no control over quality or cost. To collectively address the problem, they created early forms of consumer co-ops, buying food in bulk from farmers and selling it to members at very low markups.[9]

Cooperatives are decidedly anti-capitalist, and as such have never won ruling-class support. Legislators and churches often attacked the early U.S. co-ops as "anti-progressive" and socialist. Co-ops de-centralized profit and passed savings on to consumers, which private businesses viewed as anti-business practices. In 1859, the Rochdale Cooperative responded by devising a system whereby goods were sold at a higher markup, or even at close to market prices, and the surplus was divided among the members. This practice allowed for a margin of profit that not only covered the cost of operation, it kept the peace with surrounding non-cooperative businesses. This became an accept-able market solution, and it is perhaps the most lasting contribution from the Rochdale Cooperative model.

As the labor movement grew increasingly strong in the United States, organized industrial workers sought labor rights, including a reasonable length to their workday. Momentum for this kind of orga-nizing grew, and in 1886, thousands of workers united and marched to demand an eight-hour workday. This was the famous May Day strike in Chicago. Strikes such as this were met with governmental repression, which made workers more hostile and violent, culminating in the mar-tyrdom of some important labor leaders. It was not until many years later, in 1938, that the Fair Labor Standards Act instituted an eight-hour day. Today May Day continues to be celebrated as International Workers' Day throughout the world.

## Cooperatives Sweep America in the Early 1900s

The first large wave of American consumer co-ops was supported by active labor organizations, including unions, equity societies, and workers' leagues. By the early 1900s, union members had started a number of consumer clubs and co-op wholesalers. The wholesalers helped these clubs to open co-op storefront outlets. By 1920, more than 2,600 consumer co-op stores, most located in small towns, were grossing as much as $260 million a year.

In the late 1800s, a group that called itself the Grange created wholesale cooperatives using the Rochdale approach of selling goods to members at a low markup. The Grange cooperatives organized the first purchasing and marketing co-ops for farm equipment and ma-chinery, and even organized cooperative banks. These banks allowed farmers to buy needed farm equipment and later helped them to form political alliances with urban workers. Grange cooperatives were successful at creating political, economic, and cultural connections among members. Even today, Grange cooperatives continue to work to support economic development in rural communities and to offer hubs of community and social activity in towns across America.

The rapid development of the cooperative movement in this era made the progressive thinkers of the day hopeful that an alternative system would take the place of ever-expanding market capitalism. This sentiment led many state governments to institute pro-co-op legislation, in many cases, because they did not want to pass up an opportunity to show support for something that was both popular and economically viable.

## World War I and the Depression Era

World War I brought a contradictory economic dynamic into play in America. On the one hand, new jobs created more income for women and minorities. On the other hand, food prices skyrocketed, the result of the major export of food to feed both soldiers and starving allies abroad. Despite the growing economic need for cooperatives, with the rise of industrial coalitions of wholesalers, manufacturers, and bankers, the consumer co-op movement began to collapse. The postwar economy and the Great Depression, which began in 1929 and lasted through the 1930s, left many cooperatives bankrupt.

During the Depression the federal government's New Deal program proved helpful to rural Americans; the Rural Electrification Act of 1937 established the first large-scale electric utility cooperatives for agricultural operations. This profound change lit up rural life.

Thousands of farm cooperatives were established under the New Deal, with the goal of improving the quality of life of tenants and small farmers by resettling them on group farms located on government-owned land, where they could farm more efficiently using modern tools and techniques. However, many of these communities proved short-lived, as a result of undercapitalization and resistance from unsympathetic, conservative opponents.[10] Historical accounts indicate that the government's intervention only resulted in limited improvement.

Some of the large farmer co-ops formed during the Depression did manage to survive, but only to be absorbed by the very industries that they had been formed to resist. They had united to fight the power of agribusiness, but once they became large bureaucratic organizations, they were indistinguishable from other corporations. Some of these farm co-ops, such as Sunkist Orange, still exist as financial entities, but their members have virtually no input into their governance, making them co-ops in name only.

Another new type of "self-help" cooperative arose during the Depression when large numbers of unemployed workers gathered to barter their labor for products. In California, for example, farmworkers exchanged their labor for a portion of the food they harvested. These self-help co-ops also received support under the New Deal, and there seemed to be potential for growth. However, they were undermined by other government programs, weakened by internal struggle, and ultimately fell apart.

## Food Trends after World War II

World War II saw a decline in the popularity of co-ops, and under McCarthyism, co-ops were viewed as anti-American. The U.S. government, burdened by the war and its aftermath, overlooked the needs of rural populations. Industrial and chemical companies that had received support during the war now reinforced a growing agricultural/ chemical industry that was at odds with small farms. Large machines, new chemical fertilizers, and pesticides increased levels of food production over the short term, forcing farmers to engage in monoculture and amalgamating small farms into larger businesses. Monoculture called for expanding areas of arable land at any cost and ignored the knowledge, experience, and values of small farmers. Unable to support themselves, people in rural areas grew discouraged and migrated to the cities looking for work, a migration that further undermined existing rural co-ops.

Perhaps the most significant post war food trends were the growth of supermarkets across the country and the increasing preference for packaged groceries over the farm-fresh food that retail co-ops offered. New refrigerated trucks, walk-in coolers, and freezing and canning methods allowed food to be preserved and transported over great distances. At great expense, farm co-ops were forced to convert their operations to include processing and packaging.

By the 1950s, the connection between farmers and consumers had weakened tremendously. New mechanized farming methods alienated farmers from their own products. Large supermarkets disconnected consumers from farms and from food itself. Family farms began to be taken over by large-scale, vertically integrated industries (such as DuPont and Monsanto) that supplied a chain of companies producing farm products. The resulting revenue, which previously would have gone to farmers, now benefited corporations and contractors. This revenue was, in turn, used to purchase more farmland—today, these powerful companies continue to buy up farms. Their intense use of vast acreage drenched with harmful chemicals strips the soil of nutrients; all to maximize corporate profit in the guise of increased productivity.

Suburban consumerism in the 1950s, with its big cars and isolated nuclear families, offered little connection to the co-op movement. The ways that American people purchased and consumed food also changed radically. Given the longer shelf life, processed, packaged, and canned foods were in high demand. Corner grocery stores, bakeries, and butchers were replaced by one-stop grocery stores that offered an array of packaged foods. Poorly paid cashiers replaced the full-service clerks who had previously displayed products and wrapped purchases. People shopped once a week instead of every day. Supermarkets were able to purchase in bulk and advertise sales. Small businesses and co-ops simply could not compete. Only the large producer co-ops like Sunkist, with corporate-sized backing, survived, and they did so by marketing frozen and canned products aimed at the new consumer.

Despite the new competition from supermarkets and large monoculture farms (or perhaps because of it), a small but significant group of people grew concerned and responded with efforts to maintain the connection between food production and its consumption. By the mid-1950s, there was some indication that farmers and consumers were, once again, eager to join forces and reclaim "real" food. This group would later form the basis for the modern food cooperative movement.

## History of Food Cooperatives in the San Francisco Bay Area

The Bay Area has long been sensitive to food and food-related issues. In San Francisco, the first food co-op, the Cooperative Union Store, opened in 1867. Although it closed shortly thereafter, by the 1880s, many other new co-ops had opened in the Bay Area, including a co-op warehouse in Oakland called the Rochdale Wholesale Company.

In 1933, a wave of "self-help" cooperatives worked to save surplus produce that was rotting in California's fields due to Depression-era unemployment. Their efforts were supported by then-governor Upton

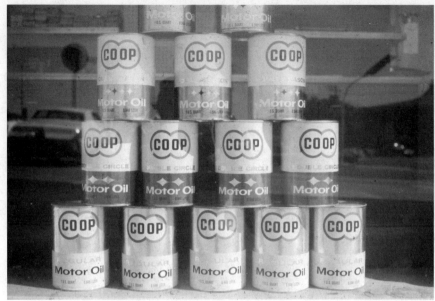

Consumer Co-op of Berkley, 1976. Photo by David J. Thompson.

Sinclair, who endorsed food co-ops in his 1933 program EPIC (End Poverty in California).

A quiet but effective enthusiasm for food co-ops continued to grow, and by the 1940s, there were many small consumer co-ops scattered across California, particularly in the San Francisco Bay Area. Buoyed by progressive politics, co-ops in California continued to be active even during the difficult years of World War II. As the growing American food industry began to control the prices and the quality of food, activist consumers in the Bay Area mobilized in great numbers to form cooperatives and regain their relationship to farms and food, as well as engaging in other progressive political action.

## The Consumer Cooperative of Berkeley
One of the most successful U.S. food co-ops, the Consumer Cooperative of Berkeley (CCB), started in the 1930s, when a food-buying club and a Finnish group called the Berkeley Cooperative Union joined together to open a small cooperative store to supply quality food at affordable prices. CCB members had close ties with the labor movement, and the store did well for twenty years. When supermarkets spread across the country in the 1950s, the CCB opened several supermarket-sized

Pacific Grove, CA, 1983. Photo courtesy of David J. Thompson archive.

co-ops in California. These markets were stocked by their own co-op warehouses, which purchased produce directly from California farmers. This arrangement both empowered farmers and provided a steady supply of fresh produce to CCB consumers.

Serving several cities in the San Francisco Bay Area, the CCB implemented the Rochdale principles of member education. They employed an on-site nutritionist to offer food-related information to shoppers and distributed literature that educated people about the adverse effects of agribusiness policies on public health and the environment. Educated and empowered, CCB members united to lobby for food labeling and other consumer-oriented policies. The CCB ran a successful business for several decades.

In spite of its rapid growth and economic success, the CCB's internal organization had begun to deteriorate by the mid-1980s. Struggles among board members destabilized the organization's administration, and without a strong administration, the workers came to feel mistreated and disempowered. Confused staff and uninformed members had no platform for reconnecting with the board. Members became apathetic and antagonistic, as management stripped them of their democratic control of the co-op.[11] Spirited activism was replaced by poorly attended symbolic meetings. The CCB did rally briefly after drastic measures were taken to restructure its membership, but it rapidly waned again. Despite a proposal that would have transformed the CCB into a hybrid model jointly run by consumer members and worker members, the CCB closed its doors in 1987, having flourished for almost fifty years and having set a powerful example for other food co-ops.

> *"It also shows the importance of education: there is no school in America where managers can study how to run a cooperative"[12]*
> —Paul Rauber

Palo Alto Consumer Co-op, Palo Alto, CA, 1978.
Photo courtesy of David J. Thompson archive.

## "New-Wave" Food Cooperatives

A new wave of cooperatives emerged in the 1960s, this time driven by the vigor and enthusiasm of the post war baby-boom youth of America. These new-wave cooperators were not members of unions or workers' leagues, and they did not see Rochdale as their model—although they did follow many Rochdale principles. This new wave of cooperators had their own brand, a new vision of a street movement that sought a social transformation that went beyond economics.

In the 1960s, the youth of America were restless, energetic, and politically active, making this era one of the most idealistic and creative in U.S. history. Disenchanted by the unpopular war in Vietnam, a war that had been created by global capitalism and funded by big industry, many young people "dropped out" of a society that seemed to offer nothing worth emulating. They wanted to replace consumerism, greed, and a "hawk" mentality with a world of sharing and harmony. Energized by a leadership of socially aware artists, musicians, activists, and ordinary people, a new decentralized food system spread across the country.

Young activists wanted to implement a new vision of food and justice. This "new wave" of cooperators envisioned a totally new food distribution system—for the people, by the people—a democratic system that would provide high quality untainted foods at below supermarket cost. The system they envisioned would offer whole foods that were nutritionally superior to the packaged foods flooding American markets. Although food, a basic necessity, was a powerful starting point for social change, their revolutionary vision included not only food co-ops, but also a larger network of independent cooperatives, both wholesale and retail, including food-buying clubs, storefront shops, bulk-food warehouses, cafés, restaurants, bakeries, bookstores, print shops, daycare centers, and more, all mutually supporting each other. Ultimately, they saw this alternative network taking economic control away from the irrational and profit-hungry "Establishment" and putting it back into the hands of "the people."

Old-wave co-ops like the CCB had been products of economic uncertainty, but the new-wave cooperators were the product of economic boom. For old-wave co-ops, growing membership and increased patronage had been symbols of success, but when they tried to maintain their cooperative principles while using corporate business models that valued growth and centralized governance, they suffered from the same problems that they had tried to avoid.[13]

The new-wave cooperators had a different vision, one that valued decentralized governance and the direct participation of individual members. They strove not only to ensure the availability of healthy affordable food and to create jobs, but also to advance social change that would bring back the personal and communal touch that had been lost in food production and consumption. Their goal was to create a sustainable food system for all people.

As co-ops and food-buying clubs opened in university towns, they educated participants. Young people across the country began to appreciate food differently, understanding its origins, seeing its connection to other aspects of the economy, and linking food choices with consumer power. One way to do this was to reconnect two alienated but allied groups: rural farmers and urban shoppers.

Food activists—including Frances Moore Lappé, Joseph Collins, Michael Jacobson, and Ralph Nader—educated the urban public about the potential for a new politics of food. These activists were also influenced by works by environmentalists, including Rachel Carson, who had published a book called *Silent Spring*, documenting, for the first time, the massive negative impact of agricultural chemicals.[14] Later activists wrote about the way in which agribusiness had seized family farms in the United States, and how land in "Third World" nations, rich with natural resources, was being systematically destroyed by U.S. government policies, leaving these countries unable to feed their own people. Agribusiness was exploiting the fertile land in developing nations by economically rewarding farmers for cultivating luxury crops for the elite and for export. These luxury crops replaced traditional staples that had once been traded locally. Food activists explained that food scarcity was not created by overpopulation in these nations, as the mainstream media suggested, but by the unequal distribution of the available food.[15]

In America, farmers were forced to abandon their diversified fields and overproduce single crops to keep up with inflation. Overproduction lowered wholesale prices. Farmers were encouraged, even forced by a lack of alternatives, to sell surplus monoculture crops cheaply to livestock farmers and to the growing meat industry, which aggressively marketed its products as "high quality" protein. Small farms were disappearing at an alarming rate, leaving fewer sources of high quality food products. The new-wave cooperators were committed to reversing the trend, first by educating themselves, and then by educating the public about the benefits of bringing back real food.

The new food activist message was that the American diet, with unhealthy amounts of grain diverted to the meat industry, led to world hunger by depriving people around the world of basic staples, while making American people overweight and sick. In her book *Diet for a Small Planet*, Frances Moore Lappé argued that a plant-centered diet could eliminate world hunger. According to Lappé, a healthy and balanced diet can be achieved by eliminating animal products and including more grains, legumes, and produce, thereby making sustainable food available to everyone. Put another way, if more people ate beans, there would be more beans to feed more people on a healthier planet. Activists like Lappé were the new role models, persuading the youth of America to examine their daily food choices. Eager to change their ways of cooking and eating, the new cooperators were ready with new recipes to save the world.

César Chávez during UFW's grape boycott. Photo by Jocelyn Sherman

While food cooperatives were expanding in urban centers, California's farmers and farmworkers were uniting and educating themselves about their rights and raising public awareness about the harmful effects of agrochemicals on the land and on workers. Farmworker activists like César Chávez and Dolores Huerta organized farmworkers into a group that later became the United Farmworkers union, or UFW, advocating both for worker safety and for consumer food safety. These activists taught farmworkers and consumers to cooperate and protest powerful agribusiness corporations using nonviolent resistance. The farmworkers' campaign to make America aware of the immense injustice done to workers by agribusiness spread across California and throughout the nation.

> "Who gets the risks? The risks are given to the consumer, the unsuspecting consumer, and the poor work force. And who gets the benefits? The benefits are only for the corporations, for the moneymakers."[16]
> —César Chávez

These new leaders also advocated democratic decision-making processes for workers' organizations and nonhierarchical community building. New-wave cooperators and farmworker groups learned from one another about democracy in the workplace and in their personal lives. Everything personal was now political.

In this climate, food co-ops were no longer isolated, and because they were not alone, they did not have to be large to be effective. The slogan "Small Is Beautiful" encouraged people to find power in small groups. The new wavers united to examine waste in food production and distribution. They questioned the quality of the food advertised with manipulative commercials, sold in big supermarkets, and eaten in isolation in front of TV sets. The goal of new-wave food cooperators was to bring food back to the people and the people back to their communities to share it in a meaningful way.

New-wave "food outlets" sprang up all over the United States during the late 1960s and early '70s. Aiming to build a local economy with new values, some co-ops organized as clubs, and others as stores. Some people prepared and sold foods, while others provided food storage and transport. Some even cooked food to give away for free! Some started in the northern states, and some in the South. Many were clustered in Minnesota and California, particularly in the San Francisco Bay Area. At their peak, these new-wave food systems connected with one another, coast to coast, buying food directly from farmers and making deliveries across the nation. Loosely known as the Food System, these food co-ops became a central part of a larger countercultural movement toward economic utopia.

Influenced by this new wave, old-wave co-ops also experienced a renaissance. They began to pay more attention to their members than to growth. However, there still remained distinct differences between the two types of co-ops, particularly in their selection of food and in their staff. While old-wave co-ops sold supermarket-style packaged food, new-wave co-ops sold fresh and bulk foods. Old-wave co-ops hired paid staff and had better paid managers, while the new-wave co-ops recruited volunteers or had workers who received negligible recompense, all of whom co-managed the co-ops democratically, often with direct customer participation.

The growth of the new-wave food cooperative movement stimulated a number of small farmers to organize and to cooperate with consumers, especially in northern California. A new rapport grew among small farmers, urban farmers markets, and food-buying clubs. This was a win-win situation for both the new-wave food co-ops and the farmers, the former obtaining fresh food and the latter having

César Chávez (holding cup) with United Farm
Workers. Photo by Jocelyn Sherman

better control over pricing. Purchasing food directly from the farmers made it possible for the co-ops to have some input into what the growers produced. Co-op members requested chemical-free food and the whole food items desired by different ethnic groups—and the farmers responded with supplies. Co-op members took frequent trips to the local small farms to bond with those communities and to gain an understanding of their work and the ways of the land.

New-wave food co-ops acted politically to support farm initiatives that helped small farmers gain control of their land. New-wave co-ops also allied with organized farm labor and actively supported the longstanding lettuce and grape boycotts called for by UFW, under the leadership of César Chávez. Some co-ops publicized their actions by placing information in their produce aisles, explaining that they had chosen not to sell boycotted food items because farm owners were making profits by denying farmworkers decent working conditions. Consumers in turn showed their support by boycotting these products. By 1970, the pressure of the ongoing boycotts resulted in contracts that provided significant improvements being signed between farm owners and UFW. Consumers had demonstrated the political and economic power of their food choices.

## Notes

1. Margaret Mead, ed., *Cooperation and Competition among Primitive Peoples* (Gloucester, MA: Peter Smith, 1976), 248.
2. Ibid., 250.
3. Howard Zinn, *The Indispensable Zinn: The Essential Writings of the "People's Historian,"* ed. Timothy Patrick McCarthy (New York: The New Press, 2012), 6.
4. Oren Lyons and John Mohawk, eds., *Exiled in the Land of the Free: Democracy, Indian Nations and the U.S. Constitution* (Santa Fe, NM: Clear Light Publishers, 1992), 228–30, 242–51.
5. International Co-operative Alliance, "Co-operative Identity, Values & Principles" (Geneva, Switzerland: International Co-operative Alliance, 2005), http://ica.coop/en/whats-co-op/co-operative-identity-values-principles.
6. Ibid. The ICA intends to periodically update the seven principles. Many co-ops use modified versions of the Seven Principles.
7. Zeuli and Cropp, *Cooperatives*, 15.
8. Ibid., 16.
9. Florence Parker, *The First 125 Years: A History of Distributive Service Cooperation in the United States, 1829–1954* (Chicago: Cooperative League of the U.S.A., 1956).

10. Paul K. Conkin, *Tomorrow a New World: The New Deal Community Program* (Ithaca: Cornell University Press, 1959), 326–31.
11. Michael Fullerton, ed., *What Happened to the Berkeley Co-op? A Collection of Opinions* (Davis: Center for Cooperatives, University of California, Davis, 1992), vii.
12. Paul Rauber, "Decline and Fall of Berkeley Co-op," in Michael Fullerton, *What Happened to the Berkeley Co-op?*, 17.
13. Paula Giese, "How the Old Co-ops Went Wrong," *Storefront Extension*, 1974, 4–6.
14. Rachel Carson, *Silent Spring* (New York: Houghton Mifflin, 1962).
15. Frances Moore Lappé, *Diet for a Small Planet*, 20th anniversary edition (New York: Ballantine Books, 1991).
16. From the film *No Grapes* (United Farm Workers, 1992).

Consumer Co-op of Berkeley, 1979. Photo by David J. Thompson.

# CHAPTER 2
# THE PEOPLE'S FOOD SYSTEM

## The Food Conspiracy

THE SAN FRANCISCO Bay Area has long been a ground for experimentation and exploration. Since the Gold Rush, people have come here seeking freedom and opportunity. In the 1960s, as political activism swept the country, young people poured into the Bay Area to escape mainstream culture, explore new possibilities, and recreate society.

At this time, a group called the San Francisco Diggers opened a "free store," which was collectively run by volunteers and gave away food and other basic goods. In addition to feeding the hungry and giving away things, the Diggers spread social anarchism and street activism through "spontaneous happenings" or events with active public participation.[1] Inspired by the free store, other grassroots organizations explored new economic models. One of the most successful of these was the Bay Area Food Conspiracy.[2] According to one source, the Food Conspiracy started in 1969 in Berkeley.[3] However, San Francisco was where the Food Conspiracy was destined to grow. By 1973, the Food Conspiracy in the Haight-Ashbury alone had hundreds of household members.[4]

In addition to buying food together, members of a Food Conspiracy group socialized and shared meals, child care, and housing. They envisioned a fully alternative lifestyle that would replace wasteful, meat-centered diets and processed food with healthy whole food shared in a community environment. To support a plant-centered diet, Food Conspiracy members popularized ethnic alternatives such as miso, tofu, and tempeh, which most supermarkets did not stock at the time.

> *"The buying clubs . . . provided people access to healthy and affordable food, which was a political necessity in an era when grocery stores preferred to stock Cheese Whiz and TV dinners instead of tofu and fresh organics."[5]*
> —Carly Earnshaw

Food Conspiracy members exchanged recipes and shared meals. They learned the virtues of chemical-free foods from farmers who had rediscovered organic agricultural techniques. Local and seasonal food practices that are popular today have their roots in the early Food Conspiracy, as does California cuisine, which grew out of a fusion of ethnic recipes and the plentiful fresh whole foods available in the San Francisco Bay Area.

One of the main attractions of the San Francisco Bay Area has always been the diversity of its cultural traditions. People from all over the world have brought their food cultures and shared them with others. The Alemany Farmers Market on Bayshore Boulevard in San Francisco was established in 1947 to meet the need for a steady supply of fresh staples. The market also connected consumers directly with farmers to the benefit both of city dwellers (who paid lower prices for their purchases) and of the nearby farmers (who received higher prices for their goods). The market became a major supply station for families and restaurants and was a regular weekend stop for Food Conspiracy members. Many of these farmers began to offer organic and/or pesticide-free produce, as interest in these items grew. Even today, with many other newer farmers markets in the Bay Area, the Alemany market continues to thrive.

Many people at this time lived in group households that became known as communes. Members of a commune often shared a common spiritual or political belief and pursued a lifestyle of peaceful, nonviolent social change. They bought, prepared, and enjoyed their food together. It was a natural step for groups like this to join a food-buying club, and two or three communes were enough to form a Food Conspiracy group.

> *"You don't need your grocery store.
> A grocery store takes up at least four
> hours a week of the average adult's
> time. In return, it numbs his mind with
> background music, tempts his pocket
> with end-aisle displays, lures him with
> advertisements and makes him walk past
> thousands of items he doesn't want in
> order to find the few he came to buy."[6]*
> —Lois Wickstrom, "How to
> Start a Conspiracy" in *The Food
> Conspiracy Cookbook*

How a Food Conspiracy group was started varied on the basis of the needs of particular neighborhoods. A typical Food Conspiracy in the Haight-Ashbury district of San Francisco might start with a group of people meeting to share a meal. This was a time when Food Conspiracy groups often started as informal buying clubs that got together in members' homes. An experienced "conspirator" from an existing Food Conspiracy group would explain the routine of ordering, buying, and dividing food, as well as the philosophy behind these practices: purchasing good quality whole food, promoting cultural unity, breaking down isolation, regaining autonomy from the mainstream economy, and educating one another about food-related socioeconomic issues. It was not just about getting less expensive food, but about sharing food. It was philosophically important that each Food Conspiracy remain small, intimate, and personal. "If you cannot walk to order your food, you should start a new neighborhood Food Conspiracy!" was the mantra.

Each week, at a potluck dinner hosted by a Conspiracy household, food orders were taken. Weekly orders usually included seasonal produce, cheese, and eggs, whereas bulk dry foods were only ordered on a monthly basis. Often when members were sharing a meal, someone would raise an issue, for example, why a certain food item was unavailable. Others might circulate the date and location of an upcoming civil disobedience action and encourage people to participate. The group would discuss these issues in a way that allowed the space for everyone's voice to be heard, with decisions reached by consensus, a model in which the majority does not rule, dissenting voices are heard, and a compromise is reached that everyone can live with. Tasks within the group were allocated based on personal ability, and jobs were often rotated so that responsibility was shared. Someone did a job for a while and then found someone willing to take over and trained that person. As Food Conspiracies spread, they became effective and empowering ways to educate communities in self-governance.

Young Rezz Sacharoff standing in front of the Haight Community Food Store, 1974. Photo courtesy of Matundu Makalani.

# ⊚Chilaquiles⊚
## A PERFECT FOOD CONSPIRACY POTLUCK DISH

Not all Food Conspiracy members were vegetarian, but everyone agreed on the value of a plant-based diet. Everyone brought a dish that was made with fresh, local ingredients that everyone could enjoy. I frequently contributed chilaquiles, a favorite with my fellow conspirators.

Chilaquiles is one of many recipes in Mexican cuisine that uses dry, stale tortillas. The dish can take a number of forms, from a soup with tortillas floating on top to a hearty casserole like this one. This casserole can be made with tomato or tomatillo sauce, cheese and/or beans, or with tofu as described here. Modest ingredients create a substantial meal for a large group of people.

- 4 cups chopped tomatoes (fresh preferred, but canned ones are OK)
- 2 tablespoons corn or olive oil
- ½ cup finely chopped onion
- 1 to 2 fresh jalapeno or serrano peppers, seeded and deveined, and finely chopped
- 3 tablespoons finely chopped cilantro leaves
- 3 to 4 tablespoons water
- 1 teaspoon salt
- 1 dozen corn tortillas (dry, stale tortillas are best)
- 2 tablespoons canola, corn, or olive oil
- A few additional tablespoons, or as needed, canola, safflower, or olive oil
- 1 cup firm tofu, drained and crumbled
- 2 cups shredded Monterey jack cheese, queso fresco (Mexican fresh cheese), or a meltable vegan cheese
- Chopped fresh cilantro leaves for garnish

First make the Mexican tomato sauce (or Salsa Roja). If fresh tomatoes are used, place them in a pot of boiling water for a few minutes until their skins split. Then transfer them to a bowl of cold water. When they have cooled, peel them and cut into small chunks.

Heat the oil in a saucepan and sauté the onion for a few minutes. Add tomatoes, peppers, cilantro, water, and salt. Cook for five minutes, stirring to blend the ingredients. This will make about 4½ cups sauce. Salsa Roja can keep for a week, if refrigerated.

Preheat the oven to 350 degrees. If the tortillas are not dry and stale, place them in a single layer on a middle rack in the oven. Bake them at 350 degrees for 15 to 20 minutes or until they become dry, but not crisp. Then put a teaspoon of oil in a frying pan and lightly fry the tortillas one at a time on both sides to soften them. Add more oil as needed, but just enough to moisten the pan. Do not allow the tortillas to become too oily or too crispy. Remove to paper towels to drain any excess oil. Cut the tortillas into 1½-inch-wide strips and set them aside.

Lightly oil the bottom of a 9-x-14-inch casserole dish. Layer the ingredients as follows: spread a cup of the Salsa Roja evenly on the bottom. Cover the sauce with a layer of half of the tortilla strips. Cover the tortilla strips with the crumbled tofu and then spread a cup of cheese over the tofu. Then continue the process with another layer of sauce, tortilla strips, and cheese. Distribute the rest of the sauce to cover dry spots. Lastly, sprinkle the rest of the cheese on top.

Cover the casserole with aluminum foil and bake at 350 degrees for 25 to 30 minutes. Uncover and bake for a few minutes more until the top is golden brown. Cool for a few minutes, cut into squares, and garnish with fresh cilantro leaves right before serving.

Makes 6 to 8 servings

Recipe adapted from *The Ethnic Vegetarian Kitchen* by Shanta Nimbark Sacharoff.[7]

On Saturday mornings, designated Food Conspiracy members went to the Alemany Farmers Market to buy fresh produce. Some members learned ways to cook produce directly from the farmers, building an inclusive sense of community. Other weekly staples, such as cheese and dairy, were picked up from wholesalers. Later, at someone's garage or at a donated public place, the truck was unloaded and the food separated into individual household orders by designated Conspiracy members. Come pickup time, people received what they had ordered, occasionally with surprise substitutions.

The monthly bulk dry-goods order, known as the "Great Divide," required more organizing than the weekly produce order. Some Conspiracies included non-food items such as light bulbs, soap, shampoo, pet food, and kitchen items in their monthly order. Even without computers and cell phones, it all worked out quite efficiently. Of course, there were the usual problems associated with any volunteer-run organization, including some people taking on too much work and other folks not carrying their weight. Once in a while, there might be a tragedy in a Conspiracy household, such as a needy "guest" taking off with the money before the person responsible for the bank run had made the deposit, but for the most part things ran smoothly, despite the fact that there were no written bylaws or formalized policies.

At the height of the San Francisco Bay Area Food Conspiracy, members saved up to 40 percent on food bills by switching from supermarkets to Food Conspiracies.[8] Members of communal households also saved on rent by sharing homes, building a sense of community among housemates that was absent in nuclear families. While living together, housemates bought, prepared, and shared food, yet retained their personal freedom.

Food Conspiracies were educational as well, as members shared food-related information. For example, research was conducted into the nutritional virtues of unfamiliar ethnic foods. People who knew how to cook unfamiliar and/or seasonal foods showed other members how. Sharing delicious ethnic dishes at communal meals easily converted newcomers to the Conspiracy's plant-centered diet, and sharing food built a sense of community.

Food Conspiracies also became grassroots organizations for social and political action, often distributing pamphlets with the news about farmworkers' strikes and boycotts of certain foods. Some volunteers ran soup kitchens to feed the hungry. Members shared gardening and other homesteading skills. Cooperative child care, alternatives to public school, and women's support groups all coalesced at these gatherings, as well. Uniting people—by drawing them together around sharing food—in an urban environment was perhaps the most important contribution of the Food Conspiracy.

## From Food Conspiracy Clubs to Community Food Stores

As Food Conspiracies grew larger, members began to discuss more efficient ways to distribute food and serve everyone, not just members. Opening storefronts seemed to be the way to go. At the time, other U.S. Food Conspiracies were converting to storefronts, the majority of which were concentrated in Minnesota, Wisconsin, Massachusetts, New York, and California. In the San Francisco Bay Area, people also drew inspiration from other collectively run small businesses.

The initial mission of these new stores was to make healthy food available to a larger section of the population than could be served by the small health food stores of the day. Ultimately, in San Francisco and across the country, the vision was to create a worker- and consumer-controlled economic base to replace the corporate food chains that had long dominated the American food system.

Replacing food-buying clubs with more stable storefront locations was also better suited to the needs of Food Conspiracy members, who were now getting older and starting their own families. Although their

Noe Valley Community Store, 1970s.
Photo by Ed Buryn; courtesy of Lourdes Weedy.

lifestyles had changed, Bay Area's creative people still had affordable housing, so they could live on minimal income. Most Food Conspiracy members were idealistic and wanted to operate the stores as a food distributor with unpaid staff. They continued with their jobs and family duties, but still found some time left over to volunteer at the co-op, thus combining their personal lives with their food politics. For these people, a stable location with a set shift was better than an erratic Food Conspiracy schedule. Although some Conspiracy members felt that opening stores compromised the community's grassroots values, the original intent of expanding into stores was not to make a profit or to create jobs, but to maintain the food distribution aspects of the Conspiracies, to stabilize schedules and manage costs, and to have a high enough margin to cover the rent.

> *"The Food Conspiracy had a lot of women involved; in fact, I think that most of the highly involved people were women. . . . Men and women worked side by side and treated each other well for the most part. The storefront seemed to attract more men. It was sexier. It had a face . . . and there was the status of being 'in charge.'"*[9]
> —Betty Harrison

## Community Food Stores and the Support Collectives

The first community food store to open in San Francisco was Seeds of Life (in Spanish: *Semillas de Vida*), in 1973. It grew out of a food-buying club that a church had organized and supported. The store was opened in the largely Hispanic Mission District of San Francisco by a group of people who managed it collectively. Seeds of Life sold many traditional Latin American food staples that could not be found on the general Food Conspiracy list. Some store workers began to bake bread for the store in the back room, a service that later inspired a business called the People's Bakery. With the success of Seeds of Life, other Food Conspiracy members began to open collectively run food stores in various parts of the Bay Area, some of them close to existing Food Conspiracy buying clubs. Existing stores helped new ones get started, and prospective shoppers, many of them Food Conspiracy members, volunteered at the new stores. Once the stores were open and reliably stocking basic food items and fresh produce, members started to shop there instead of ordering food through their Conspiracy.

By the mid-1970s, flourishing Food System community food stores and their supporting venues included the Bernal Heights Community Corners Food Store, the Noe Valley Community Store, the Good Life Grocery, the Seeds of Life, the Cooperating Warehouse, Veritable Vegetable, the Red Star Cheese Collective, Merry Milk, the People's Bakery, and the Yerba Buena Spice Collective—all clustered around San Francisco's Mission District. Rainbow Grocery, which was originally opened by members of a spiritual community, later joined. Around the same time, the Haight Community Food Store, Other Avenues Food Store, and the Inner Sunset Community Food Store opened their doors in the western part of San Francisco. The Flatlands, Uprisings Bakery, and Ma Revolution opened in Berkeley at about the same time. Other business collectives emerged to support the stores, and their names were as colorful as their missions—they included *Turnover*, a newsletter collective; the Honey Sandwich, a day-care center; People's Refrigeration, a refrigeration-maintenance collective; People's Trucking; and Left Wing Poultry, a collective selling eggs wholesale.

To set themselves apart from the old-wave food co-ops that still existed, store workers consciously refrained from calling their stores "cooperatives." They used the term *community food stores* to emphasize the fact that the stores were open to everyone, in contrast to the earlier member-based Food Conspiracy. The existing crew often voted in new workers and everyone was a "collective member."

Each collective held regular meetings to discuss business and community matters, including food selection, staff expansion, and community events. In most collectives, the meetings were open to everyone and decisions were made by consensus. There were, however, some groups that used a majority-rule voting model. While many collectives and stores advocated decentralized, group decision-making over centralized governance, no one at the time would have described the situation at his or her workplace as anarchy.

When they first opened, most stores were staffed by volunteers, with an occasional paid position for the worker who picked up food from wholesale outlets. Workers were informally recruited from among the shoppers, and the workers who had regular shifts made the daily operating decisions. Most stores kept their markup very low—just enough to cover the rent and spoilage. There was almost no division between paid and unpaid workers, and the help of regular shoppers was always welcome.

> *"In those days, it was not an uncommon event for a volunteer worker to stop cashiering at the Haight Community Food Store and ask a long line of shoppers to help unload the delivery truck. The shoppers would temporarily leave the line to assist."*[10]
> —The author's memories

## The Rise of the People's Food System

Each collective workplace, be it a store or a bakery, had its own rules, and each was independent from the others. As a group, the collectives were united by a strong philosophical commitment to community and a common mission of not-for-profit food distribution to and for "the people." A group of workers from among these stores and collectives in the San Francisco Bay Area began to meet regularly to discuss shared goals, eventually calling themselves and their collectives the San Francisco Bay Area's People's Food System (PFS), and their motto was "Food for People, Not for Profit."

The People's Food System representatives met monthly to exchange ideas and to unite the rapidly growing number of PFS collectives. These meeting were originally called the Joint Meetings, then later the Inter-Collective Meetings and the All Co-op Meetings. Attendees discussed how to connect with suppliers, how to get the community more involved, where to open new venues, and so on. At first, meetings rotated among the various collective locations, but later they were held at the locations where the most members attended. Meetings, open to all community members, were often laborious and generated more disagreement than accord, but the goal was always to develop tools to bridge ideological differences and bring a sense of unity to the collectives.

Individual PFS collectives were financially independent, but they supported one another ideologically and worked together to gather resources for a variety of new projects. Established collectives helped new stores with money and support. Experienced workers shared their skills by training staff at new venues. Sometimes PFS member collectives supported venues that not all members used. For example, at one point, PFS businesses jointly funded the Honey Sandwich, a child-care center located near the Noe Valley Store, which was almost only used by PFS parents who worked in the area.

San Francisco Cooperating Warehouse workers, 1970s.
Photo courtesy William Saltman and Nina Saltman.

## The Success of the People's Food System

At the height of the People's Food System, between 1976 and 1978, there were approximately two dozen community food stores and supporting collectives. Although they followed some of the international principles of cooperatives, PFS workers remained reluctant to identify their workplaces as co-ops. They had witnessed the dissolution of the Consumer Cooperative of Berkeley, which made a distinction between shoppers and staff, as well as between the workers and management, and also lacked member participation. The community food stores had no desire to repeat those particular mistakes. Instead of working to become a chain of supermarkets, most community food stores adhered to the value "small is beautiful." Keeping food sources local, with community members handling distribution, meant that everyone could participate and the businesses would not outgrow the communities they served. On the other hand, many workers in leadership roles had visionary dreams of replacing the entire agribusiness system with the People's Food System.

> *"Some had a vision of a people's food system that would completely bypass the large corporations and supermarkets that now supply the food most Americans eat. Organic farming collectives would grow the food, and trucking collectives would bring it to the city to be sold at community food stores."[11]*
> —Morris Older

The People's Food System primarily attracted white youth, although minority groups, immigrants, and women with young children also joined the PFS, because they were attracted by its democratic governance. They felt it was a system that could be empowering and could unite minority groups. Spontaneous networks sprang up, enriching their surrounding communities. For example, a group of women hosted fabric workshops in their homes, enrolling students through the stores. Other members created nonprofit businesses or taught healthy living classes. One of the first women's centers in San Francisco was located in the Haight-Ashbury, not too far from the Haight Community Store. The PFS stores became community playgrounds and crossroads, where members nurtured one another's visions.

> *"The People's Food System gave us a community empowerment of performance through self-help."[12]*
> —Lori Campbell

The community stores also offered education for alternative lifestyles. A vegetarian diet was no longer considered a restrictive diet fad for "health nuts," but was accepted as a mainstream healthy choice. Frances Moore Lappé's wildly popular *Diet for a Small Planet* became the food activists' guidebook, showing that individual consumer food choices had the power to affect global change. Many stores gave workshops on gardening and vegetarian nutrition and offered cooking classes. Mainstream America was becoming more and more suspicious of the meat monopoly, and many people were ready for a change, something that was more feasible in the few places where alternatives were more easily available, including the San Francisco Bay Area.

Consumers became more aware of the deteriorating quality of commercial food products and more conscious of the massive quantity of harmful chemicals being dumped on farmland by large companies like Monsanto and Dow. The PFS disseminated information addressing this issue through food-activist publications and its own newsletters and pamphlets. Information that could affect consumer choices and educate shoppers about current food politics issues and upcoming rallies was often disseminated in creative ways, for example, in the form of product labels and bread loaf wrappers.

Community groups that addressed social issues, such as women's rights and the civil rights of minorities, supported these collectively run food stores, as both shoppers and allies. In just a few years, from 1973 to 1977, a time when the American economy was chronically depressed, the PFS distributed millions of dollars' worth of food and reached thousands of households. This was clearly a major success both economically and politically.

In the late 1970s, PFS workers were still dedicated to "Food for People, Not for Profit," but a changing economic climate made wages an issue that had to be addressed. Landlords did not offer commercial space rent-free, and the small markup at most of the stores was not enough to pay workers wages. Some of the workers firmly resisted paying wages; they considered food distribution to be a political action that would be compromised by paid labor, and they feared that raising prices to cover labor costs would mean that only the affluent would be able to afford the food, defeating the purpose of serving more people by replacing buying clubs with stores. While others felt the stores could not survive without paid labor, the workers faced economic pressures of their own, and many could no longer afford to contribute their time for free.

Paid or not, PFS workers enjoyed the egalitarian nature of their work, and took pride in the fact that their labor made healthy food accessible to a growing number of people. The stores (and some collectives) held business meetings that were open to the public, fostering a sense of community. Nonetheless, the day-to-day operation of the stores and other venues was increasingly managed by a core group of workers. The question of wages remained unresolved and, at the end of the day, was addressed differently by each store and collective.

## Toward an All-Collective Unity

As the People's Food System grew, the vision of a unified food system gained popularity. Some leaders from the Cooperating Warehouse and Veritable Vegetable were at pains to build quality human relationships with growers, food producers, and other warehouses across the country. Others held Joint Meetings to discuss forming an economic alliance with common system-wide procedures. The idea of unifying the system was greeted enthusiastically by the collectives, and attendance at these Joint Meetings increased.

Members who regularly attended the Joint Meetings decided that the first step toward unification was to adopt a Criteria Statement that established what was necessary for a particular collective to be part of the PFS. Initially, these were good-faith efforts to define membership in the People's Food System and to bring about a sense of cohesion. The Criteria Statement was published in the September 1975 issue of *Storefront Extension*, the PFS's first newsletter, presenting a long list of requirements to qualify as part of the People's Food System.[13]

This Criteria Statement was the first printed attempt to define the mission of the People's Food System. An accompanying statement said: "We are in position of needing to place limitations on the number and structure of the groups we agree to work with. . . . We see a main part of our work as understanding and struggling against an oppressive capitalist profit-oriented economic system. We are being careful not to support those groups that oppose the struggle against capitalism and those groups that are unwilling to struggle."[14]

The Criteria Statement was debated in many Joint Meetings. Regardless of attempts by some individuals to limit membership or to certify members on the basis of the PFS mission statement, many venues, such as the Cooperating Warehouse, served any and all "not-for-profit" groups that seemed legitimate. Eventually, a series of forums was set up to allow members of all of the collectives to discuss the unity of the People's Food System. At an April 1976 conference, attended by seventy PFS workers, a proposal in favor of "democratic centralism" with an elected Representative Body (RB) was approved in the hope of unifying the system.

The RB consisted of two representatives from each PFS collective. In the hope of defining and uniting the PFS, the RB formulated a doctrine called the Basis of Unity (a modified version of the aforementioned Criteria Statement), which was approved by most active collective members. The Representative Body also elected a Steering Committee to take on the task of unifying the PFS. Although the committee was elected without objection, many collectives opposed the task force.

Some of these groups' original meeting notes indicate that the Steering Committee was composed of people with strong personalities, and that some of them resorted to rhetoric in an effort to centralize the power of the PFS.[15] In the May–June 1976 issue of *Turnover*, a later PFS publication, a collective was defined as "a group struggling to become non-sexist, non-racist, and anti-capitalist."[16] However, not all members embraced this definition, and many felt that the effort being made in this "struggle" was difficult to measure. Many felt that in the debates around the need to meet these standards, the original issue of food distribution was lost. Some of the philosophical exchanges between various Food System members, on these and other matters, appeared in PFS newsletters.

The first PFS publication, *Storefront Extension* had been launched in 1974 to share news within the PFS. Later, the PFS published an expanded monthly magazine called *Turnover*, addressing food issues and politics, with articles on topics ranging from nutrition to global food concerns. The editors consciously addressed the economic impact of agribusiness on people in the United States and other nations. For example, one article exposed the sale of Nestlé infant formula to Third World mothers as a replacement for safe, traditional human breast milk, pointing out that in many cases the use of formula led to illness and malnutrition. The article advocated a boycott of all Nestlé products.[17]

*Storefront Extension* published a special issue on sugar, exposing both how seductive ads lured children to over-consume hazardous sweets and the ways that monocropping sugarcane destroyed valuable land that had once been used to produce healthy staples. This issue was popular, and a revised, updated version that included certain clarifications appeared in *Turnover*, in 1976. A Spanish translation, "El Azucar," was published by *Turnover* in 1977.[18]

Cover of *Turnover* (newsletter of the People's Food
System), July/August, 1976. Artwork by Rich Tokeshi.
Courtesy of newsletter collective and Pam Peirce.

*Turnover* also reported on labor issues, including the farmworkers' grape boycott. It also included articles about issues that were not directly related to food co-ops, such as a story about the Symbionese Liberation Army kidnapping the wealthy heiress Patty Hearst and demanding free food for the hungry in exchange for her release.[19] *Turnover* illustrated the passionate food politics of the day with creative essays, recipes, drawings, poems, and cartoons.

Despite the fact that the various PFS collectives had not achieved philosophical unity, they all agreed in principle about the need to combat the rising power of capitalism, not only in the food industry, but also in areas that included the corporatization of mainstream media and corporate control of the housing market. In addition to creating and supporting an alternative food network, the PFS dedicated energy to other community causes, co-op housing and community radio among them. In the Haight-Ashbury neighborhood, both a commercial-free, independent community radio station and a storefront dedicated to finding housing for newly arrived homeless people were founded and staffed by groups of PFS workers. Ways to support these causes were discussed at the stores and in All-Co-op Meetings and were publicized in PFS newsletters. The PFS also organized several national conferences attended by farmers and co-ops across the nation to address ways to jointly combat growing agribusiness practices. In September 1975, more than one hundred people from California, Washington, Oregon, Arizona, and Canada attended one of these conferences.

As an alternative to mainstream celebrations marking America's bicentennial, the PFS organized the People's Bicentennial Celebration (PBC) in July 1976. This event mobilized thousands of people in the Bay Area to reclaim basic revolutionary ideals from the corporate "fiefdom" that had taken them hostage. The entire PFS network promoted this event, providing food, making banners, and distributing literature at various PFS stores. Members marched, placards in hand, singing songs of camaraderie and freedom. Anti-war activists, tenants' rights organizers, gay rights advocates, farmworkers, and other minorities rallied for this event.[20]

On another occasion, the PFS formed a united front in solidarity with the elderly Chinese and Filipino residents who were to be evicted from the International Hotel in San Francisco. They spread news of the eviction and called in workers to set up solidarity night shifts.[21] Clearly, the People's Food System had a good deal of potential for affecting political and social change.

```
STORE DIRECTORY

    Community Corners    826-9850    47 Powers
    Flatlands            841-4390    1853 Ashby (Berkeley)
    Food for People      922-1581    c/o 773 Cole St. #10
    Haight               752-5278    1920 Hayes
    Inner Sunset         c/o 564-6342 1224 9th Ave. (soon to open)
    Ma Revolution        548-6761    2525 Telegraph Ave. (Berkeley)
    New Oakland          832-9472    2710 Park Blvd.
    Noe Valley           824-8022    1599 Sanchez
    Other Avenues        731-9567    4035 Judah
    Rainbow              863-6835    3159 16th St.
    Seeds of Life        826-6814    3021 24th St.

SUPPORT COLLECTIVES

Amazon Yogurt            826-0900    3030 20th St.
Earthwork                648-2094    The Farm: Army at Potrero
Honey Sandwich Day Care285-8209     3056 24th St.
Left Wing Poultry   408-779-2234    13465 Watsonville Rd. Morgan Hill
Merry Milk               285-9771    3030 20th St.
Newsletter               285-8817         "
People's Bakery          826-2488         "
People's Refrigeration 826-0900           "
Red Star Cheese          826-0900         "
SFCW (Warehouse)         648-7717    155 Barneveld
Uprising Bakery          841-7108    2575 San Pablo Ave. (Berkeley)
Veritable Vegetables     826-0996    3030 20th St.
Yerba Buena              826-2774         "
```

```
TURNOVER/NEWSLETTER COLLECTIVE            BULK RATE
3030 20TH STREET                         U.S. Postage
SAN FRANCISCO, CA 94110                      PAID
                                        San Francisco, CA
                                         Permit #11478
```

List of People's Food System stores and support
collectives, 1974–76. Courtesy of the *Turnover*
newsletter collective and Pam Peirce.

## Internal Conflicts in the Struggle for Unity

As the organization continued to rapidly grow, and new collectives
were formed, internal struggles started to surface within the PFS. All
members wanted to sustain growth, but there was no clear agreement
about its direction. Some Representative Body leaders wanted to expand the PFS into underserved communities and create a larger socialist system of representative democracy. Others were strongly opposed,
preferring to build more small, autonomous collectives that operated

with direct democracy. There were a number of members who had strong feelings about the issues but did not take a position.

As the collectives grew and began to pay their workers, each of them had to define its own structure. They all embraced equality, but, with a mix of trained and new staff, some paid, some not, this became increasingly difficult to achieve. As the discussion at RB meetings came to center on democratic centralism, with a focus on the Basis of Unity Statement, the concerns of individual collectives were no longer adequately addressed.

The PFS Steering Committee elaborated a decision-making process and established a central PFS fund to assist new and existing venues. With input from some collectives, it revised the Basis of Unity Statement. To do this, the Steering Committee requested that representatives from each collective take the RB's proposals back to their collectives for discussion and return with feedback. This did not always happen; some stores, Other Avenues among them, were simply too busy trying to keep their doors open. As a result, instead of creating a strong, stable unified system with the participation of all collectives, the proposed Basis of Unity Statement served to aggravate the growing discord between the RB and some collectives.

## Growing Conflicts Regarding Diversity in the Food System

At one point, an RB member made a proposal "to unite the food system around politics" and "form a group of the most politically conscious people to deal with" unresolved issues.[22] This patently contradicted long-cherished values of equality among workers. Those who did not accept the RB's methods of fighting sexism, racism, and classism were severely criticized at the meetings. At one point a proposal was made that a group from the RB talk to workers from a certain store and "straighten them out."[23]

Some members walked out of these tense meetings.[24] Others stopped going to the meetings altogether, feeling that their voices were not being heard and that the "democracy" was missing from the growing "centralism."[25] Many wanted to return to the Joint Meeting structure that they felt had been more successful.[26] In mid-1977, Rainbow Grocery and the Noe Valley Community Store dropped out of the Representative Body. However, the collectives that stopped going to RB meetings continued to be part of the People's Food System—for example, they continued to be served by other PFS venues, including the Cooperating Warehouse—and there was genuine, open discourse among the workers from different collectives.

A recurring point of discussion was the question of diversity. Despite vocal affirmative-action policies, some members felt strongly that the PFS was still mainly run by a "white counterculture" that was guilty of latent sexism and racism, and that "Third World" people were not adequately represented on PFS staffs. Although the PFS theoretically supported women's rights, many women working in the system felt that their basic needs, such as child care, were not sufficiently addressed. Individuals in leadership tried to be sensitive, but all too often it seemed like leadership roles for minorities received little more than lip service.

In response to these concerns, the RB adopted an assertive policy that encouraged hiring from marginalized groups, such as gays, migrants, and other minorities, making these practices part of the 1976 Basis of Unity Statement. Some collectives felt that these were important issues for progressive workplaces and wanted even more aggressive affirmative action. Other collectives, however, continued to struggle with basic issues, including whether or not to pay their workers, and were not in a position to take a stand on who should or should not be hired.

In the late 1970s, similar ideological struggles were also unfolding among new-wave food co-ops elsewhere in the United States. Started mostly by white middle-class college youth, and inspired by the civil rights movement and other progressive struggles, the new-wave food movement strongly advocated diversity and wanted to reach out to minorities, but working in a heterogeneous group in a non-hierarchical structure is never simple. The PFS was far from alone in its struggle to reconcile its social values with the business of running a co-op.

## Gunfire Signals the End of an Era

In 1977, a shooting at a PFS meeting had serious repercussions. There are various versions of this event and many theories as to why it happened, what led up to it, and why it brought a sudden breakdown to what had been the successful and rapidly proliferating People's Food System. What follows is but one attempt to synthesize the incident and its aftermath.

As the PFS implemented its broad affirmative action policies, its pool of workers became more diverse, bringing in more ethnic minorities, women, and even ex-prisoners on parole. At this time, progressive people recognized prisoners as an oppressed group, and some collective members working as part of a movement to improve prison conditions in California petitioned the PFS to hire inmates on parole, particularly political prisoners. Some of these new hires came to the PFS via a parole program that granted early release to prisoners who had outside job offers. As part of this plan, Willie Tate, one of the San Quentin Six (a group of prisoners linked to a highly publicized case involving the murder of three prison guards and three inmates, including George Jackson) was released and employed at Ma Revolution Food Store.

Veritable Vegetable, the PFS produce wholesale collective, had hired some former inmates from another group, called Tribal Thumb. According to some sources, Tribal Thumb had a powerful and charismatic leader named Earl Satcher.[27] Tribal Thumb and Satcher allegedly had a role in the assassination of a prison activist associate of Tate's.[28] This meant that members of former inmates from two separate groups were working in two different Food System venues at the same time.

Unlike the labor activists, most PFS workers did not have a party affiliation or follow specific leaders. Figureheads did emerge from time to time, many of them selfless guardians who were articulate in their promotion of co-op values and offered stewardship by example. However, there were some leaders who were intent on advancing their own personal agendas, and some vulnerable collective members who followed them. Although not a member of a PFS collective, Satcher appears to have assumed such a role. By hanging out with Veritable Vegetable workers, Satcher was able to gain access to and influence over a few Tribal Thumb members employed by the co-op. This entrée would later gain Satcher even more access to the People's Food System, when members of a political, pro–armed struggle group called the White Panthers, some of whom worked in the PFS, began to sympathize with Tribal Thumb. The White Panthers ultimately helped Tribal Thumb gain influence in a number of PFS collectives.[29]

A former PFS worker recalls that some of these new recruits were suspect because they showed little interest in healthy food or collectivity, but seemed primarily focused on gaining power within the system.[30] Some workers feared that Tribal Thumb loyalists would help

Satcher take over the PFS, a concern that Tribal Thumb supporters dismissed as elitist. Tensions around this new group mounted within the PFS. Workers who wanted to focus on food distribution felt that the PFS had abandoned the issue to devote a large amount of collective energy to creating a polarizing political platform.

A special conference of all PFS members was held on April 17, 1977, to discuss, among other things, the much-debated critique of the Basis of Unity Statement and democratic centralism. While the meeting was closed to workers who were not currently part of the PFS, some specific people who had been active in the PFS in the past were invited to observe. A Tribal Thumb member who worked at Veritable Vegetable brought along a few uninvited Tribal Thumb members who were not part of a PFS collective to act as observers. A heated conflict erupted between some PFS workers and Tribal Thumb members during the meeting, and the rest of the conference was spent discussing the disruption. Most participants felt that the Veritable Vegetable worker who had brought the Tribal Thumb visitors should be expelled from the PFS, or at least reprimanded and suspended.

A special meeting of the RB was held on April 26, 1977, to address Veritable Vegetable's failure to discipline those who had interrupted the previous meeting. "During the meeting it became clear that VV was not willing to struggle in a principled manner, but it was attempting to manipulate the meeting . . . and being generally disruptive."[31] Veritable Vegetable's status in the PFS was to be decided after a break. "During the break gunfire broke out."[32] In somewhat confusing accounts of the event, it has been reported that Satcher was waiting outside with another man and two Doberman guard dogs and tried to attack Tate, who was unarmed. After the shooting and the tumult that followed, Earl Satcher was found dead, and Willie Tate was critically wounded.[33] Several PFS workers were arrested and charged with first-degree murder. While some charges were dismissed for lack of evidence, some individuals did serve jail time.[34] Satcher's murder was never solved.

It is important to pause here to assess the feelings expressed by those who were present at this violent event. Some PFS members dismissed it as simply a stage set for an existing feud between two rival groups of prison inmates who were associated with two different PFS workplaces. Others saw the event as the result of an accumulation

of unwise decisions made by a "guilty white" leadership that hasti-
ly recruited new workers and then allowed them unearned authority. One member stated with certainty that the incident occurred
because counterintelligence agents had infiltrated the Food System.
Underground media at the time reported evidence linking Satcher to
agents involved in an FBI plans to provoke violence within the PFS as
part of a counterintelligence program called Cointelpro.[35]

Members who saw the event as the result of internal conflict
within the PFS laid the blame on a weak leadership. They felt that the
Representative Body had been ineffective in delegating important
tasks to other collectives and had relied too heavily on the Steering
Committee, which had usurped so much power that it "did not need
outside cops."[36] The PFS had become so factionalized and fragile by
this point that it was ripe for being trampled by an outside force.

*Turnover* carried a brief report about the shooting in its Spring
1977 issue, requesting defense funds for those implicated. Although
*Turnover* was dedicated to addressing a variety of global issues, it was
apparently unable or unwilling to examine or explain the growing
problems within the PFS. No recorded account from within the PFS
fully addresses the unification struggle; only a few anecdotal exchanges
between collectives reference the issue.

> "Turnover *wants feedback. . . . They do
> a lot of political discussion and struggle
> as they work on each issue. [It] is the
> only continuous educational tool in the
> food system and needs feedback."*[37]
> —From an RB meeting's
> notes, December 1976

## The Demise of the People's Food System

After the shooting, the Cooperating Warehouse was broken into,
and then closed for a while. Many workers were afraid to return to
work. Police questioned the leaders, and some workers felt intimidat-
ed and left the Bay Area. When the Warehouse reopened and meetings resumed, the Representative Body declared a boycott of Veritable
Vegetable for being "uncooperative," but some stores within the system

continued to work with VV nonetheless. The PFS warehouse would remain open and continue to serve the existing collectives until a flood in 1981 destroyed much of its stock. However, by then the PFS as a whole had lost its focus and was in rapid decline.

The Cooperating Warehouse finally closed in 1982, and one after another, with only a few exceptions, PFS retail food stores and venues followed suit. Outlets, Red Star Cheese among them, closed soon after the Warehouse. Other PFS venues soldiered on; the Uprisings Bakery, for example, survived for more than a decade, finally closing in 1997.

After 1982, most storefronts folded. The Inner Sunset Community Food Store and the Noe Valley Community Store managed to hang on for more than a decade, closing in 1995 and 1996 respectively. In 2016, of the original People's Food System stores, Rainbow Grocery and Other Avenues are still going strong. The Veritable Vegetable warehouse has also survived, and is thriving as a wholesale distributor, although the business is no longer a collective. Good Life Grocery in Bernal Heights is also doing well as an employee-stock-ownership retail business.

## How and Why Did the PFS Fold So Suddenly?

There were, of course, many passionate discussions involving PFS workers from across the Bay Area as the system fell apart, but these talks were not well documented. The mainstream media either ignored or misrepresented the shooting incident. It is notable that of the underground media, only the *Berkeley Barb* printed anything.[38] Accusing Satcher and Tribal Thumb of "fanning the flames of provocation," the *Berkeley Barb* seemed to place most of the blame for the destruction of the PFS on Tribal Thumb, citing its alleged connection with the FBI.[39]

PFS members themselves analyzed at great length the internal conflicts that had brought about the dissolution of their dream. They examined the role played by their collective action or inaction and the outside influences on the leadership, and attempted to understand why most PFS collectives were unable to survive the shooting incident. Some blamed the demise of the PFS stores on members' lack of business skills. There were, in fact, many business-savvy people in the organizations, and some of them went on to work for successful business ventures, but while they were in the People's Food System, they didn't place enough emphasis on the daily business of running a network of retail food stores. Poor management and petty theft were also blamed for the closure of some of the stores.

> *"At that time, people were more interested in political discourse than running a business . . . as a result the business suffered."*[40]
> —Nina Saltman

Others felt that the unmanaged organizational growth had led to the lack of a coherent joint vision. In a few years, the PFS had grown tremendously, bringing chaos along with its collective enthusiasm. Growing unresolved ideological differences among various collectives undermined the integrity of the organization as a whole and left it ripe for collapse.

> *"The Peoples Food System grew too fast to incorporate the human dimension."*[41]
> —Adam Raskin

An article in the *Bay Area Directory of Collectives* claimed that the PFS descended into an irresolvable power struggle between Marxist/centralist advocates and hippie/anarchists.[42] However, not all of the Marxists in the PFS were centralists, and not all of the hippies were anarchists. Clearly, as its membership became increasingly diverse, the PFS struggled unsuccessfully to create a joint organizational mission, but this conundrum alone does not explain why only a few stores were able to survive.

The PFS faced other significant dilemmas, including unresolved issues of racism, sexism, and classism among the workers. A sticking point for the new-wave cooperators in general, and the PFS groups in particular, was a recurring inability to resolve communication problems among their diverse populations. PFS groups made a genuine effort to bring diversity-related issues to the surface and worked hard to try to sort them out. Sincere efforts were made to learn new tools of nonviolent communication from other progressive community movements and leaderships. Some of these attempts succeeded, and others failed. Our society has become even more multicultural in the meantime, and current co-ops continue to face these communication concerns. Specialized co-op professionals and workers continue to embrace the same nonviolent communication skills, while adding new tools and a renewed vigor to bringing about more harmonious and diversified workplaces.

Some people also mentioned the isolation of the PFS from other businesses as a source of the dissolution. By building their own network, the collectives set themselves apart from other health food outlets and businesses. When their wholesale warehouses closed, the stores, which had no relationship with non-PFS vendors, found themselves at a disadvantage. These stores were neither able to rapidly create the necessary rapport nor to obtain needed credit from the outside business community.

There were also many challenging external influences that left the PFS vulnerable to dissolution. Some of these were political or economic, but others were the result of social changes that put pressure on cooperative businesses. Even without the ideological divisions that weakened the organization, the PFS would have had to change dramatically to survive. For example, in the early 1980s, under Reagan, federal government policies increased aid to agribusiness interests at the expense of farmers and small businesses. As a result, the number of small farms and retailers in the United States declined precipitously, and in this climate even the most stable consumer co-ops foundered.

The U.S. economy in the late 1970s and the '80s did not favor small business. Small food stores, with their limited markup and uncertain suppliers, struggled more than most small enterprises. Even during a healthy economy, mom-and-pop stores rarely prosper, despite low overhead and family labor. Nationwide, the new-wave food co-ops suffered from declining income, rising rents, and internal struggles. The PFS was not the only organization that found it difficult to meet these challenges; faced with the same socio-economic circumstances, opposing parties acted out a similar scene at the Minneapolis food co-ops.[43] Many food co-ops across the United States closed their doors during these years.

In California, Proposition 13 (limiting property taxes) became law in 1978, setting off a real-estate boom that benefited landlords. Rents for storefronts doubled, as did rents for apartments and houses. As the cost of living rose, collective members could no longer afford to work or live in the Bay Area, and PFS stores could no longer find reasonable rents or an affordable labor force.

In the 1980s, the new "natural food" industry began to co-opt what the PFS had created. The PFS had spawned a strong new public awareness of whole food and its health benefits. In response, there was increased competition among health food retailers as natural food went mainstream. Supermarkets began to carry many foods formerly found only at health food stores and co-ops. Commercial manufacturers labeled their products with words like "natural" and "whole" to attract customers. Soon large chains of specialty groceries, such as Whole Foods, Wild Oats, and Trader Joe's, began to take over the niche that co-ops had served.

In the Bay Area, a strong backlash against radicalism also undermined not just the co-op movement, but social justice efforts overall. There was ample evidence to support the idea that activist organizations like the PFS were targeted and disrupted by outside forces. Similarly, organized groups questioning government support for agribusiness began to get unfavorable media attention as political views in the country continued to swing sharply to the right.

Consumers changed too. Where in the past money had been scarce, but time plentiful, now educated young people in California had all-consuming, well-paying dot-com jobs. Though they might support the idea of small farms and co-ops, they had no time to contribute. What they did have was money, and they wanted their food fast and easy. In the techno-boosted Bay Area, "webvans" began delivering organic foods to those who were chained to their computers. Former food activists were now busy with activism in other areas, including environmental work, and it seemed for a time that there was nothing being done in the realm of food activism. There were still some food co-ops in California, but the food movement as whole had fallen dormant.

Even in the light of all of the other influences, everyone interviewed for this book who had witnessed the demise of the People's Food System still believes that were it not for the violent events of April 1977, the PFS would have evolved differently. More storefronts and outlets could have been saved. And perhaps the People's Food System could have been transformed into another form of organization, such as a group of independent franchise venues like the current Arizmendi Association (discussed in Chapter 7).

> "Outsiders did not know about our fragility. . . . Without their infiltration and the shootout event, the People's Food System would have ended more organically."[44]
> —Morris Older

## What Became of PFS Workers and Shoppers?

With more than a dozen food stores and venues, the PFS reached many people throughout the Bay Area. For a while, with the demise of the PFS, and the growing conservatism across the United States, the radical food co-op community became disconnected, but the downfall of the system did not mean the end of progressive ideals.

A small but committed group of workers stayed at the remaining stores; some early members still work in Bay Area co-ops. Many workers from the stores that closed found work at the surviving stores. The dormant resources gave rise to new businesses. For example, two local businesses that grew out the demise of the Food System were People's Goods and Tool Store and Other Avenues Food Store. People's Goods and Tool Store took over the defunct Haight Community Food Store's space, selling tools from catalogs. (Currently, that storefront is the home of the Freewheel Bike Shop.) In the Outer Sunset District, Other Avenues drew the support of the Inner Sunset community shoppers who had supported the now closed Inner Sunset Community Store.

Many members of the food system transferred their self-reliance, their ability to question authority, and their experience of working collectively—all of which they had learned during their years in the food system—to their personal and professional lives. These cooperators found they had become "radicalized" in the process of changing the food distribution system, a personal transformation that left them unable to return to the status quo. Some former PFS workers extended their "pure" food passion into food-related businesses, some moved to the land to establish organic farms, some joined environmental groups or progressive nonprofit organizations in the public health sector, and still others went to school to study the "green economy." A few even went to Washington, DC, to promote legislative changes for sustainable agriculture.

Devoted co-op shoppers who were involved in food-related activism through the PFS were left with nowhere to shop—but that didn't last long. Some bought their food from the remaining stores, while others purchased directly from farmers markets, which became very popular in the 1990s and have continued to spread. Another retail food-buying option became available when the Community Supported Agriculture (CSA) groups started a program selling shares in farm produce to individuals and households. Many of the farms involved make weekly household deliveries of CSA boxes.

A variety of food-buying clubs have sprung up around the country, especially in rural communities, where people continue to demand local organic food at reasonable prices. When asked how these food clubs are different from the older Food Conspiracies, a member mused that they no longer use the clipboard to gather orders. Instead, they use the internet and credit cards. However, they arrange their food pickups and deliveries cooperatively, just as was the case in the past. She added that they also share their food resources, including community gardens and recipes, in the way the old Food Conspiracy did.[45]

The role of food in building communities has not been lost in the San Francisco Bay Area. Many former PFS members continue to eat together and participate in local food activism and movements for social change. The PFS dream of communal food sustainability lives on in the proliferation of group activities, such as the urban gardeners who reclaim public spaces and work with neighbors to grow local foods and plants. Parents partner with community groups to get organic food for families and schools. Community organizations, such as Food Not Bombs, support a vital food and justice movement working to obtain fresh food for underserved urban and rural populations. Others campaign to improve the nutritional quality of institutional foods served as public school lunches, public hospital menus, and in jails and juvenile residences.

## The Legacy of the People's Food System

Three still thriving collective businesses that survived the demise of the People's Food System are described in the following chapters. But the PFS was about much more than business; it was also a vehicle for social change. Its legacy is widespread and enduring. The People's Food System left a strong imprint on the next generation of the Bay Area food and justice movement, which remains proactive and powerful, and continues to focus on the well-being of the people and the planet. The meaningful dialogue among collectives, consumers, farmers, and farmworkers that was initiated by the PFS continues today within what remains a progressive social force. It has spawned a number of politically and economically active food-related communities that defy the escalating international food conglomerates and defend the rights of food workers, consumers, farmworkers, and small farmers.

In particular, the PFS created awareness among a vast number of people and encouraged them to seriously question the growing global monopoly of food corporations, chemical companies, factory farms, giant production centers, and extravagant distribution networks. The PFS was a forerunner in widely publicizing the possible adverse effects of genetically modified and pesticide-ridden foods on the health of consumers, farmworkers, and farmers. New data continue to arise that deepens these concerns, and today, farmers and consumers around the world are actively resisting agribusiness and its agenda. The United Farm Workers, the union that spoke up against hazardous work conditions and unfair compensation, received active PFS support. These same farmworkers' unions are now backed by a new generation of co-op workers who join them in the struggle to advance farmworkers' rights and to address the related immigration issues.

The modern organic food movement gained recognition in the United States during the 1960s and '70s, when "natural" foods were first popularized and strongly supported by the new-wave co-ops. The PFS embraced this movement and carried it forward, as progressives in the San Francisco Bay Area became staunch supporters of green agriculture. The PFS expanded consumer awareness of the health benefits of a whole food diet, emphasizing the environmental importance of unpackaged, organic, and plant-based fresh foods. This awareness has spawned a number of new trends, including the raw food and "locavore" movements, which focus on consumption of food produced in local communities.

New-wave cooperators voiced concern about the sustainability of the modern American diet at a time when nutritionally depleted packaged foods were shipped across the country and aggressively marketed in place of fresh whole foods. A national animal rights movement advocating a meatless diet was also strong among 1970s co-ops. The PFS made healthy vegetarian ingredients affordable to people of the Bay Area, who then discovered how easy it was to cook real food with an international flare. Homemade foods began to replace the post-industrial cardboard foods. Fresh, made-from-scratch ethnic recipes became popular, as did previously unknown ingredients. This plant-centered ethnic cuisine has now evolved into healthy "fusion" cooking and a new California cuisine. The PFS can be credited with turning California into a vegetarian mecca with numerous vegetarian-friendly restaurants.

New-wave cooperators advocated and organized to mobilize public awareness around food safety issues. When PFS meetings began to drag on around topics like "whether or not to sell white sugar," study groups were formed that unveiled underlying economic, social, and health issues and educated the public regarding the nutritional and political impacts of food. Some of these topics have since affected legislative public policies, strengthening consumer interest in nutritional information, and leading to better (though not perfect) food labeling laws and practices.

The topic of wasteful food packaging was addressed by the PFS and other new-wave co-ops across the country. The practice of not using plastic bags and reusing bags and containers, which is now gaining popularity, even at mainstream supermarkets, was the rule at PFS stores. Dry goods and spices were sold in bulk, despite the fact that stocking some of these items could be cumbersome. Bulk goods, which are more ecological and less expensive than packaged foods, are still very popular at the remaining PFS businesses among people concerned about sustainability and the health of the planet.

The kind of expanded community organizing we see today was enthusiastically endorsed and popularized by the collectives and cooperatives that made up the People's Food System. At their height, food co-ops and other collectives, such as daycare centers, bookstores, bicycle shops, and restaurants, networked to efficiently support one another. Inspired by the success of the PFS, other businesses, including independent radio stations, printing shops, and art centers, adopted worker-managed collective models. To help interested people find and support businesses that shared similar cooperative values, a group published and updated the *Collective Directory,* from 1977 to the mid-1980s.

There is now a vast diversity of collective businesses in the Bay Area, many of them mentioned at the end of this book. The developments of organizations supporting cooperatives in the Bay Area— such as the Network of Bay Area Worker Cooperatives (NoBAWC), the California Center for Cooperative Development (CCCD), and the United States Federation of Worker Cooperatives (USFWC)—will also be discussed in chapter 7.

Individual transformation via food-related activism during the PFS era has also been noted by those who participated in that movement. The personal became political among food co-op workers and shoppers. After struggling with global issues, including the Vietnam War, civil rights, and nuclear power, PFS collectives and shoppers brought their politics home, focusing on the issues of everyday life, particularly what foods to buy and eat. The consensus model of decision-making was adopted in many collective households. Today newly arising housing collectives, new family structures, and intentional communities owe much of their transformative inspiration to the example set by the People's Food System.

> *"When I came into the Food Conspiracy as a young person I came from being deeply immersed in the counterculture, mostly the fight against the Vietnam War.... The Food Conspiracy and [its] offshoot organizations, i.e., women's collectives, child-care collectives, radio collectives, etc., were representative of vibrant/tangible new society formats that we were trying to create. It was a time of great hope. I carry this [vision] with me in ideas of where I spend my money, how I use resources, and how I communicate with people in the workforce bringing ideas of workers' rights."*[46]
> —Seth Harrison

The People's Food System is not gone; it has been transformed by the same people who participated in it. It has evolved into other newer progressive groups, ideas, and actions. The PFS sowed fertile seeds for the next generation of food organizers, peacemakers, and labor activists. Free lunch programs, soup kitchens, and public community gardens have grown out of the ideals of the PFS. The collective work of PFS workers continues to influence our culture and society, as we focus on issues like how to distribute healthy food to all the people, how to incorporate good food choices into public programs, and how to teach the next generation about the farms and gardens that supply our food.

## Notes

1. Carly Earnshaw, "Radical Food History," http://bit.ly/28Lbi3U.
2. In addition to the author's personal recollections and notes, much of the material used to address the Food Conspiracy and the People's Food System (PFS) was obtained from the PFS's original meeting notes, the *Storefront Extension* newsletter, *Turnover* newspaper, and personal interviews conducted in 2010–12 with the following former PFS members: Lori Campbell, Charlie Engelstein, Mary Jane Evans, Betty & Seth Harrison, Jeff Kaplan, Morris Older, Adam Raskin, and Nina Saltman.
3. Lois Wickstrom, *The Food Conspiracy Cookbook* (San Francisco: 101 Productions, 1974).
4. Nancy Grant, "Haight-Ashbury Food Conspiracy," *Communities: A Journal of Cooperative Living*, 21 (August 1976): 32–35.
5. Earnshaw, "Radical Food History," http://bit.ly/28Lbi3U.
6. Wickstrom, *The Food Conspiracy Cookbook*, 10.
7. Shanta Nimbark Sacharoff, *The Ethnic Vegetarian Kitchen* (San Francisco: 101 Productions, 1984), 126.
8. Wickstrom, *The Food Conspiracy Cookbook*, 17.
9. Author interview with Betty Harrison, August 2011. Betty worked with the Food Conspiracy and the PFS from approximately 1971 to 1975.
10. The author's personal memories of the Haight Community Food Store in 1975.
11. Morris Older, "The People's Food System," in *History of Collectivity in the San Francisco Bay Area*, ed. John Curl (Berkeley: Homeward Press, 1982), 39.
12. Author interview with Lori Campbell, June 2011. Lori worked at the Haight Community Food Store, 1975–76.
13. "Criteria Statement," *Storefront Extension* 5, September 1975, 6–7. The Criteria Statement listed 12 criteria.
14. Ibid., 6.
15. Unpublished original notes of an RB meeting, December 16, 1976.
16. "The Food System Meets," *Turnover* no. 12, 5.

17. Dahlia, "Formula for Malnutrition," *Turnover*, October 1976, 10–15.
18. "Sugar," special issue, *Storefront Extension* 8 (December 1975); "Sugar," special issue, *Turnover*, revised edition (1976); "El Azucar," supplement, *Turnover*, August 1977.
19. Vicki Raymond, "Emily and Bill Harris on Trial," *Turnover* 26, August–September 1978, 27–28.
20. Older, "The People's Food System," 40–41.
21. Ibid., 40.
22. From original, unpublished notes of an RB meeting dated December 16, 1976. Notes taken by Judy (no last name recorded) from the Inner Sunset Store.
23. Ibid.
24. Ibid.
25. Author interview with Jeff Kaplan, 2011. Jeff worked at the Inner Sunset Community store, 1975–78.
26. Author interview with Charlie Engelstein, 2011. Charlie worked at the Inner Sunset Community Store, 1975–78.
27. Imilla Cabral and Bill Wallace, "Showdown and Shootout," *Berkeley Barb*, December 21, 1978–January 3, 1979, 8.
28. Ibid., 8.
29. John Bryan, "Food Shoot-Out Communiqué," *Berkeley Barb*, May 6–12, 1977.
30. Author interview with Charlie Engelstein, 2011.
31. *"People's Food System's Statement on the Expulsion of Veritable,"* an unpublished written announcement distributed to PFS venues by the RB after the events of April 1977.
32. Ibid.
33. Imilla Cabral and Bill Wallace, "Showdown and Shootout," *Berkeley Barb*, November 1978, December 2, 1979, January 3, 1979. Investigative series on Tribal Thumb.
34. Ibid.
35. Imilla Cabral and Bill Wallace, "Get those Crazy People off the Streets!" *Berkeley Barb*, January 4–17, 1979.
36. Author interview with Charlie Engelstein, 2011.
37. From original, unpublished notes of an RB meeting December 16, 1976.
38. Cabral and Wallace, "Showdown and Shootout" and "Get those Crazy People off the Streets!"
39. Ibid.
40. Author interview with Nina Saltman, April 2011. Nina worked at the PFS Cooperating Warehouse, 1974–78.
41. Author interview with Adam Raskin, April 2011. Adam worked at the Cooperating Warehouse 1974–78.
42. "What Happened to the 'People's Food System?'" in "Reincarnation of the Rebel Spirit," *Bay Area Directory of Collectives: Listing, Map and Articles* (Berkeley: Bay Area Directory Group, 1980), 50.
43. Craig Cox, *Storefront Revolution* (New Brunswick, NJ: Rutgers University Press, 1994).

44. Author interview with Morris Older, 2011. Morris worked with the People's Food System at Uprisings Bakery, 1974–76.
45. Author conversation with Charlene Lilie, a member of a food-buying club operating in San Jose, 2012.
46. Author interview with Seth Harrison, August 2011. Seth worked with the Food Conspiracy, 1971–75.

# PART II
# THE PEOPLE'S FOOD
# SYSTEM SURVIVORS

As THE BAY Area's People's Food System weakened, a few of the businesses born out of that movement that were committed to surviving supported one another. As was discussed above, when Veritable Vegetable was boycotted as a result of internal PFS conflicts, Rainbow Grocery and Other Avenues continued to buy from them. In the years after the PFS folded, when the Noe Valley Community Store, the Inner Sunset Community Store, and Other Avenues were struggling, Rainbow offered essential advice and support. Three surviving businesses (two stores and a wholesale product outlet) remain interconnected and support one another at cooperative conferences and gatherings.

In the early 1990s, workers from Rainbow and Other Avenues attempted to create an umbrella organization, the Inter-collective Organic Union, to unite the surviving PFS member organizations. Although the union was short-lived it organized two large and successful public events in Golden Gate Park bringing together co-op workers, farmers, and supporters. Bands made up of members of the co-ops provided the music, local farmers offered food samples, and the co-ops arranged food-related activities for children. There were speeches by Dolores Huerta and other food activists, and educational literature focusing on farmworkers' rights, the benefits of organic agriculture, and the importance of food cooperatives was distributed.

Despite these attempts at solidarity, the sad fact is that a number PFS cooperatives went under in the 1990s. Inner Sunset Community Food Store folded in 1995, and Noe Valley Community Store went out of business in 1996. As noted above, by the turn of the twenty-first

century, only two retail cooperatives, Other Avenues Food Store
and Rainbow Grocery, and one wholesale produce outlet, Veritable
Vegetable, remained open.

These three businesses revitalized themselves and are now doing
well. How is it that these three survived and remain vibrant, even today? The continuing strength of the Bay Area's food and justice movement helped, as did the growing national interest in organic foods and
healthy eating, but that is not all that kept these business going, while,
one after another, the others folded. For all three, it is clear that their
success in business and food activism was, and is, largely due to 1)
strong connections with both their immediate neighborhoods and the
food and justice community at large, 2) constant attention to pragmatic business practices, 3) a clear mission to bring healthy food to the
people, and 4) a strong commitment to workplace democracy.

This is not say that these survivors are not confronted with many
of the same socioeconomic challenges faced by urban populations
across the nation. Other Avenues, for example, survived the stagnant
economy of 2005–2008, but is now losing some of its loyal customers
and staff due to the rising cost of housing in the San Francisco Bay
Area. Similarly, for the first time in years, Rainbow Grocery has had to
promote itself more assertively to respond to the rising competition
in the retail health food market. The constant efforts Rainbow and
Other Avenues make to reach out to their communities have made
both co-ops resilient, and Veritable Vegetable has remained a leader
in organic food distribution in the Bay Area, despite the arrival of new
wholesale outlets and the proliferation of farmers markets. Other food
and justice organizations and activism also survived the decline of the
1960s and '70s food cooperatives and remain alive and active in the
San Francisco Bay Area.

# Chapter 3
# Veritable Vegetable

Veritable Vegetable (VV) is the oldest major distributor of certified organic produce in the United States. From a forty-two-thousand-square-foot warehouse, VV distributes organic produce to Arizona, California, Colorado, Hawaii, Nevada, New Mexico, and New York. Dedicated to providing the highest quality organic fresh fruit and vegetables to local food co-ops, natural food stores, restaurants, schools, and corporate campuses, VV buys organic produce from more than 300 growers and supplies it to more than 400 retailers, wholesalers, and other outlets. An established leader in the expanding organic agriculture industry, VV has a long history of supporting sustainable farming and fair labor practices, values that are not commonly shared by many food distributors.

Veritable Vegetable is a women-owned company founded on principles of cooperation, participatory management, and ethical business practices—values that are similar to those of worker cooperatives, although VV is no longer a cooperatively owned business. VV's staff of more than 130 full-time workers enjoys many benefits not usually available at small businesses or co-ops. VV is proud of its use of green technologies in its San Francisco facility. These technologies are continually updated to reduce energy consumption and waste at every level of the company's operation. VV views itself as a business driving socioeconomic and environmental change, and actively participates in food justice advocacy.

## VV's Early History
Veritable Vegetable was formed in 1974 as part of the San Francisco Bay Area People's Food System, with the goal of supporting small and

midsized independent farms and distributing affordable fresh produce wholesale to PFS retail stores. From the very beginning, VV's vision was both pragmatic and political: to provide high quality, reasonably priced produce to local communities, while acting to protect farmers, farmworkers, consumers, and the environment.

Three women owners of Veritable Vegetable. Photo by Chris Adams.

In the 1970s, a growing number of farmers were rediscovering organic and sustainable farming practices and using new production techniques, but they were competing against chain stores supported by conventional agribusiness and subsidized by the government. As consumers became more concerned about the destructive effects of modern agribusiness practices on public health and the environment, demand for fresh organic food increased across America. Small and midsized organic farmers were ready to supply the products people wanted, but, with the exception of a few farmers markets, there was no stable organized supplier to bring produce of this kind to market.

At first, all of the PFS support collectives operated out of the same warehouse at 20th and Alabama Streets in San Francisco (except for the Cooperating Warehouse, which housed bulk dry goods at a separate location). The founders of the PFS collectives had a common vision: to create a large-scale alternative food distribution system that would eventually replace the corporate system. A few individuals gathered together to focus on buying and selling produce. Calling themselves the "Veritable Vegetable Collective," they formed direct relationships with local growers to bring organic produce to the PFS and other small businesses in northern California.

Like most of the People's Food System supply collectives, Veritable Vegetable started as a worker-run collective, with all workers making business decisions jointly and being paid the same wages. By the late 1970s, most of the PFS, including VV, had become extremely politicized, and the workplace was seen as a venue for social change. VV was divided into two factions. Some VV workers were strongly aligned with the like-minded leaders of the Cooperating Warehouse and took a firm Marxist view of changing society from the bottom up.

These workers were affiliated with radical activist groups like the White Panthers that advocated armed struggle to bring about social justice. They also felt strongly that VV should embrace affirmative action measures to recruit workers from diverse and marginalized social backgrounds, including former prisoners. However, they did not have tools to screen these worker applicants, let alone to train them to do the necessary work. This faction would eventually become embroiled in the political friction within the PFS discussed in the previous chapter.

Leaders of the other faction within VV had a different approach. They hoped to bring about social change solutions to concrete problems, such as reaching a group consensus for dividing work assignments and developing an effective decision-making process. They emphasized training and assessing worker performance, and focused on building closer relationships with local farmers, something that would be of service to both VV and their customer base. In pursuing this practical approach, they eschewed a rhetorical debate with the Marxist tendency.

Within a week of the shooting and the expulsion of VV from the PFS described in the previous section, most of those who had taken a hardline political approach left VV, as did some of those from the "pragmatic approach" side who had grown discouraged in the face of the collapse of the PFS. Only a few VV workers remained, and they were determined to repair their organization and carry on with their dream.

In addition, VV had lost 75 percent of its customer base and was asked to leave the warehouse that it occupied with other PFS collectives. In their effort to keep the business going, the VV workers who had prioritized VV's mission to distribute affordable, healthy produce stayed on, while those tied to a hardline political agenda immediately withdrew.

Four members of the original VV collective remained, and they were determined to keep the doors open. They approached the surviving PFS collectives and petitioned them to continue doing business with VV. Using a consensus model, VV reformulated its governance structure and gathered a new workforce. VV also returned to its focus on developing relationships with growers and on gaining new retail customers, including stores such as the Real Food Company and the Berkeley Co-ops. This allowed VV to stay in business and survive the collapse of the PFS.

> *"Many of the supply collectives and storefronts took a position informed by hardline political rhetoric. This contributed to the collapse of the Food System. Those collectives, like VV, Inner Sunset, Other Avenues, and Rainbow Grocery, that blended political awareness with practical application, continued as viable businesses long after the demise of the People's Food System."*
> —Mary Jane Evans

## VV's Rebirth

By the end of 1977, VV had moved to a larger location and hired more workers to meet a growing demand for fresh produce. Fortunately, throughout the PFS turmoil, VV had maintained a strong rapport with its produce suppliers, so while other PFS collectives were unable to remain open after the shooting and the economic downturn of the early 1980s, VV consolidated its business and began moving toward stability.

> *"In times of economic downturn, we
> tend to do well. It seems that when
> people have to curtail discretionary
> spending, they choose to eat good food."*
> —Mary Jane Evans

VV workers felt the collective had been tested and had survived, and they were inspired to rededicate themselves to their original mission. The company added a fleet of trucks, which allowed them to reach out to both more suppliers and more customers. Small co-ops such as Other Avenues that could not afford to keep their own trucks benefited from VV's new delivery service. In 1982, after several years of rapid growth, VV outgrew its warehouse space and moved to a much larger location.

> *"Business expansion was accomplished by
> rebuilding our internal worker community
> and by externally establishing a strong
> relationship with farmers and retailers."*
> —Mary Jane Evans

Steady customers and dependable suppliers helped VV to revitalize its business, but success was not without its challenges. The rapid growth left the company's leadership exhausted, and the size of the staff made traditional forms of collective decision-making cumbersome. Unproductive meetings frustrated the workers, and some of those with more experience began to be dissatisfied with the fact that all workers received equal wages. Although the higher volume of sales allowed the company to acquire a larger space and more equipment, it still lacked a comprehensive vision of how to address financial planning. Because VV had no formal structure for dealing with its fiscal difficulties, all the bookkeeping team could do was keep the staff updated regarding the business's troubled finances, and the debts were growing.

In late 1988, VV's leadership hired an outside consultant to help the business develop and institute a new organizational business structure. The consultant conducted a detailed worker survey, which provided workers with an opportunity to express themselves. The survey clearly indicated that even though the company was a collective, hardly any of the workers wanted to be owners and that there was a clear need to restructure company management.

With this information, two women who had held leadership roles in the collective, and who had signed the leases for equipment and for the building, offered to become (and were elected as) directors/owners of the business.

They took personal responsibility for the debts, instituted a well-defined differential pay structure for employees, and appointed department managers. Based on VV's earlier success, the two women were confident they could unite the staff and keep the existing network of vendors and buyers satisfied. They were right.

After its reorganization under the leadership of these two women, VV's operations rapidly recovered. Higher revenues and greater profits followed, and VV invested its surplus in worker benefits and business improvements. Even now, VV spends most of its surplus on state-of-the-art equipment and worker benefits and wages. VV's wages generally start at twice the California minimum wage. Worker morale is clearly of great importance to company leaders.

The 1990s were economically stable years for VV. More and more Americans turned to a plant-centered diet and organic food from local sources. This trend coincided with VV's improved organizational and business changes. VV grew and prospered, and was able to meet the community's demand for high-quality produce from reputable local sources.

## Veritable Vegetable Today

Veritable Vegetable, a certified B Corporation, now has more than 130 full-time employees and its 2014 revenue was approximately $49 million. VV meets rigorous social and environmental performance, accountability, and transparency standards, as defined by B Lab, a third party certifier. VV continues to actively offer women job opportunities in areas that have traditionally been the domain of men—ranging from driving trucks and warehouse work to executive leadership positions. In 2014, more than 60 percent of VV's staff was female, with women in executive and ownership positions.

Working at a wholesale produce business is physically demanding. The hours are long and some jobs require very early morning shifts, while others mean working at night in damp, refrigerated coolers. Nonetheless, knowing that their work helps to keep organic farming

sustainable and bring healthy food to more communities is deeply sat-
isfying for VV workers.

VV's management makes sure that workers receive great benefits
for their hard work. In addition to higher-than-average starting wages,
VV workers receive medical benefits and a retirement savings plan, as
well as daily perks that include nutritious catered vegetarian and vegan
meals, organic snacks, and easy-to-prepare healthy frozen foods. The
workplace has a dedicated stretching area with pads and other equipment, two nap rooms, and dark, quiet spaces with cots where workers
can rest during breaks. Obviously, workers' well-being is important
aspect of VV's successful mission.

Ownership at VV means "taking on the responsibility of running
the company and developing and carrying forward VV's original mission."[1] The company's close-knit organizational system and management structure clearly defines worker responsibilities, while fostering
clear and open communication. Business structures are reviewed regularly to make place for workers' voices in all aspects of the business.

The company has directors, managers, assistant managers, and
supervisors, all of whom are fully integrated into the day-to-day line
work and/or administrative work, making joint decisions and running
company departments. Meetings use the consensus model developed
by Community at Work, a San Francisco–based organization that
teaches group decision-making techniques.

> "As we develop our succession plan,
> we continue to explore options that
> allow us to carry our business values
> forward. We have always been extremely
> interested in the idea of employee
> ownership as a way to carry on the
> VV legacy. While we cannot currently
> define our future structure, we can
> say the decision-making process will
> carefully consider the best interests of
> all our customers, growers, and staff."[2]
> —A collective statement from
> Karen Salinger, Mary Jane
> Evans, and Bu Nygrens

## Working at Veritable Vegetable Is More Than a Paycheck

VV is a great place to work for people concerned about the environment, sustainable food systems, and social justice. We strive to improve the quality of life for our employees both in the workplace and beyond because we believe employment doesn't end with a paycheck. In addition to competitive salaries, we also offer all fulltime employees:

- *Health, dental, and life insurance for yourself and a spouse or domestic partner*
- *Employee Assistance Programs for counseling at low or no cost*
- *401(k) plan in socially responsible mutual funds*
- *Year-end profit sharing*
- *Referral bonuses*
- *Flexible holiday and leave policies*
- *Infant support benefits*
- *Commuter reimbursement*
- *Weekly in-house 10-minute massages*
- *Credit for four massages per year*
- *Boot allowance for drivers and warehouse workers*
- *Section 125 pre-tax Cafeteria plan*
- *Free vegetarian and vegan meals*
- *Access to fresh, organic juices*
- *Worker Food Program enabling staff to bring home fresh, organic produce below retail prices*
- *Field and Farm Day tours*
- *Incentives for voting in elections*
- *Extensive in-house training program*

*From Veritable Vegetable's website[3]

VV promotes sustainable agriculture by working with organic farmers and those who use biodynamic techniques to grow food in harmony with nature. Biodynamic growing techniques emphasize the interrelationship of soil, plants, and animals in a holistic system. In addition, VV educates its customers, including retail co-ops, food-buying clubs, other independent food businesses, schools, and caterers, by providing and disseminating information about the sources of its products, including where and how the food is grown.

VV offers onsite educational tours of its warehouse to the community and to people who are interested in viewing a model green facility. VV's thirty-five-thousand-square-foot space with ten coolers uses green technology to efficiently control the temperature and ensure food safety. VV's 560 solar roof panel, energy-saving ballasts, and other cooler fixtures are an investment in energy efficiency. VV diverts 99 percent of its waste from landfills by reusing, recycling, and composting. VV furniture is made from reclaimed wood, and the warehouse insulation is made from used jeans.

VV promotes the organic food industry and important organizations that foster sustainable food systems, including the California Certified Organic Farmers (CCOF), the California Food and Justice Coalition, Center for Urban Education about Sustainable Agriculture (CUESA), the California Institute for Rural Studies, and the Organic Consumers Association. VV's support takes the form of both food donations and organizational support, including participating in educational events.

Consistent with its mission of "Food for People, Not for Profit," VV contributes generously to its surrounding community. The company regularly donates organic produce for a variety of public events, including Other Avenues community events, and to nonprofit public institutions and wellness programs that serve children in the San Francisco Unified School District among them.

By providing good benefits and quality equipment to its staff, supporting organic farmers, paying fair prices, and promoting organic produce, VV has been able to remain financially sound while taking political action in support of food and justice.

### Notes
1.    Mary Jane Evans, in a written communication with author.

2.   A collective e-mail statement from Karen Salinger, Mary Jane Evans, and Bu Nygrens.
3.   "About VV: Our Team," Veritable Vegetable, http://www. veritablevegetable.com/our-team.php.

Special thanks to Nicole Mason, VV marketing and communications man-ager, for reviewing this chapter prior to publication. Additional thanks to Karen Salinger, who helped me finish this chapter.

# CHAPTER 4
# RAINBOW GROCERY COOPERATIVE

LOCATED IN THE busy Mission District of San Francisco, Rainbow Grocery Cooperative has grown to be one of the largest retail health food stores and one of the largest worker-owned cooperatives in the United States. The Mission District was historically working-class Irish and Italian, before becoming a largely Latino neighborhood. These days, with the arrival of a new generation of tech workers, it's more heterogeneous. As a result, Rainbow now serves customers from a great variety of ethnic groups and income brackets.

Situated on the edge of a busy residential community, close to San Francisco's financial district, Rainbow benefits from a steady stream of foot traffic and a stable customer base, and this is augmented by its easy access from a major freeway. Health food chain stores located nearby, including Whole Foods and Trader Joe's directly compete with Rainbow, but the co-op has survived and continues to prosper, largely due to its careful selection of product lines, emphasis on affordability, keen focus on customer service, and commitment to workplace democracy.

Rainbow's history is marked by a series of challenges met and overcome during its decades of operation, and today Rainbow workers and shoppers are confident in its secure future. Over the years, Rainbow has more than doubled its workforce from about 85 people to over 250.[1]

## The Early Days
Rainbow Grocery Store was started in 1975 by the residents of an ashram, a spiritual community that followed a Hindu philosophy of nonviolence and vegetarianism. Before founding the store, the community

purchased fresh produce from a farmers market and bulk foods from a bulk-food-buying program organized by one of its members. At the time, this member also worked at the Cooperating Warehouse, part of the San Francisco People's Food System. Inspired by the work of the PFS, he encouraged the ashram group to open a food store that would serve the community in San Francisco's Mission District, which was in dire need of a retail outlet offering healthy, "natural" food.[2]

Rainbow Grocery Co-op truck, 1990s.
Courtesy of Rainbow Co-op.

A few other community stores and wholesale outlets connected with the Food Conspiracy had already opened in other parts of San Francisco. These stores and venues formed a loosely connected association, helping one another with seed money to open new community-based health food stores and sharing mutual business skills and cooperative governance values.

Rainbow's first store was in a small storefront on 16th Street near Valencia. A diverse, increasing young and affluent community now populates the area, but at that time the neighborhood was considered "sketchy" and undesirable for retail business. Despite the odds, Rainbow soon became one of the busiest stores in the People's Food System. This was partially due to Rainbow's spiritual background, which stressed service to the community without an ulterior motive, and also because of the strong leadership of its founders, who had business experience.[3] Some of these founding members still work at the current store.

From the very outset, the workers at Rainbow had a strong, conscious commitment to serving their community and focused on acquiring the necessary business skills. These two factors would prove to be the most essential elements of Rainbow's success, buoying the store while other PFS outlets descended into political infighting.

Like other PFS stores, Rainbow opened its doors with a volunteer labor force. As it started to show a surplus (what is "left over" to share among members after all expenses and debts are paid, generally known as "profit" in the corporate world), Rainbow became the first PFS store to pay its workers, and what was initially a bare minimum wage became a reasonable living wage as the business became more profitable.

Although Rainbow was first staffed mostly by the ashram's religious community, it soon became a secular workplace with a diverse staff. Unlike other PFS venues that had to impose affirmative action on hiring, Rainbow workers employed ethnic minorities from the very beginning. To provide effective customer service, Rainbow wanted its staff to reflect the community it served. A name like *Rainbow* even seems to suggest gender, class, and cultural diversity.

Until 1976, the two founders who had signed the initial papers legally "owned" Rainbow, although the workers always considered the business a nonprofit organization. Later, Rainbow workers copied the Cooperating Warehouse model and incorporated the store as a nonprofit business. They continue to pay business taxes, because, as they discovered, retail businesses are not eligible for tax-exempt status. At this point, Rainbow was not a co-op but a collectively run business that used some of the governance tools that PFS workers had developed. Rainbow workers made collective business decisions and used profits to expand inventory and provide worker benefits.

### The First Expansion

After amassing an ample surplus in 1978, Rainbow added some nonfood inventory to the store, including items like vitamins, body-care products, housewares, books, and clothing, sold in a separate location called Rainbow General Store. Workers had anticipated an even greater surplus from these high-margin items, but the first expansion resulted in substantial losses. This trend was reversed when some skilled staff members began to attend trade shows and learn to select nonfood items more carefully, placing more emphasis on supplements than on other goods. A limited inventory of supplements and a well-trained and well-informed staff to help customers paved Rainbow's way to economic success. Today Rainbow is one of the largest retail suppliers of supplements in the United States.

## Involvement in the People's Food System

In the 1970s, when the PFS started its food distribution movement, Rainbow was actively involved. Rainbow workers connected with other PFS members at Joint Meetings to exchange news, share business skills, and acquire the tools of collective governance. However, when the PFS became entangled in political infighting in the late 1970s, Rainbow workers, observing that the PFS had no clearly articulated shared vision and that a group of ambitious people had started to harness the collective energy for their own political purposes, grew cautious. When the PFS's Representative Body and Steering Committee demanded that all stores accept the PFS Principles of Unity, Rainbow workers decided to drop out and refocus their energies on their original mission, providing healthy food to the community.[4]

After the Cooperating Warehouse went out of business, a couple of workers proposed starting a Rainbow wholesale warehouse, but the staff rejected the idea. Later on, the staff did, however, approve a wholesale division, which was owned by Rainbow, but operated by two people in a separate location. The wholesale division closed after a few years of operation.

With their business refocused, Rainbow workers remained in contact with the remaining Food System venues. For example, Rainbow continued to buy produce from Veritable Vegetable during the boycott. Because of its sound and successful business, Rainbow, which clearly cared about other democratically run businesses, was in a position to provide other PFS stores with advice and financial support during the challenging 1980s. Decades before the co-op movement vocalized its principle of "cooperation within cooperatives," Rainbow supported its fellow cooperatives as much as it was able.

Long after the collapse of the PFS, Rainbow remained a force in Bay Area food activism on both a local and a more far-reaching political level. Rainbow workers actively supported the California Farm Workers' struggle during the 1970s, as well as promoting local, small-scale organic farmers, purchasing produce directly from them whenever possible.

## Rainbow's New Digs at 15th and Mission

The 1980s were not co-op-friendly years. Rents skyrocketed in the city, making it increasingly difficult to staff small businesses. Despite previous business growth and a dedicated staff, Rainbow experienced some financial difficulty in the early 1980s. However, its tight, cooperative management and excellent customer service allowed the store to continue to grow and expand. In fact, before long, Rainbow had grown too large for its small storefront on 16th Street.

After much discussion, Rainbow's staff decided to risk moving the store to a new, much more spacious location. In 1983, Rainbow moved from its two-thousand-square-foot double storefront on 16th Street to a nine-thousand-square-foot warehouse space at the busy corner of 15th and Mission Streets. Workers who favored the expansion argued that the larger space would allow for sales and service growth. It would also be more shopper-friendly, since the new location would sell both the grocery and non-food items in a single space. Some workers were nervous about the change and wanted Rainbow to remain small. They feared that such a major expansion would undermine the collective nature of the business. According to a longtime worker who supported the move, these concerns proved unfounded.[5] After the expansion, Rainbow remained committed to the principles of collective operation and devised new governance structures for its larger location and bigger staff.

Financing the move was challenging. Although the store was financially stable, banks were not comfortable with the collective's ambiguous ownership status and were unwilling to extend loans. Rainbow turned to its community for help, raising $250,000 for the move—a huge sum at that time. Construction at the new space and the relocation of the store were financed with generous loans from customers and community members. There was, however, also a lesson learned: the collective now understood that it must clarify its legal ownership status before approaching banks for future financing.

While other PFS venues were struggling to stay open in the late 1980s, Rainbow Grocery was booming. The store increased its sales by 68 percent in the first year at the new Mission Street location. In 1988, the *San Francisco Bay Guardian* ran a cover story on Rainbow with a large photo of its forty-four workers. Rainbow was recognized as "A '60s business that prospers in the '80s." The article looked at a group of the Bay Area's then successful alternative "bumblebee businesses" that practiced "openness, honesty, sharing and service" and focused on "right livelihood."[6] Rainbow was selected as a model for this article, a major acknowledgment of its success during an era when most remaining Bay Area independent businesses that had been built in the 1960s and '70s were struggling to survive.

> *"We have a strong sense that we're not just shoveling out food. . . . We're giving a kind of dignity to the whole process . . . to expand the awareness of the people who shop here."*
> —Stanley Sacharoff, a Rainbow worker during the 1980s who was one of the people interviewed for the *Bay Guardian* story

Rainbow's success was mainly due to the dedication of its workers, who integrated modern business tools that proved effective, while maintaining the principles of their original mission. With efficient business practices and a reasonable markup, the workers were soon able to accrue a substantial surplus. They shared this profit in the form of higher wages and their first group health insurance plan.

Under the new business model established for the Mission Street location, Rainbow was separated into two distinct sections; the grocery store sold food, and the general store sold supplements, body-care products, books, clothes, and gifts. Each section had a sub-organizational structure and made its own daily operating decisions. Major decisions affecting Rainbow as a whole were made at joint meetings of all of the workers from both stores. Although this model proved successful, the workers expressed a growing desire for a more cohesive and integrated business structure. Eventually, the workers created a board of directors, which met regularly to implement policy decisions and, with substantial worker input, make financial decisions for the business as a whole.

As the business grew, the workers adapted without compromising the politics behind their product choices. They expanded both the bulk product department and the fresh produce department, while maintaining their inventory of high-margin items, such as supplements and body-care products. The store took a stand on issues of sustainable agriculture and remained active in the Food for Justice movement in the

Bay Area. In the 1990s, Rainbow helped to establish production and sale standards for organic food cultivation and certification in California.

Rainbow's workers maintained strong ties with the neighborhood they served by bringing in products that were popular with various ethnic communities. The store hired local minorities and, unlike other PFS stores, even in its early days Rainbow had developed effective tools for addressing organizational issues related to the diversity of its staff.

In the early 1900s, Rainbow participated with other food cooperatives in creating the public Harvest Festivals in Golden Gate Park. Rainbow also took part in local celebrations, including Cinco de Mayo and the Gay Pride Parade. A longtime Rainbow worker recalls onsite Spanish/English language exchange classes meant to help workers to better communicate.[8]

After a decade of growth at the 15th and Mission Street store, even this large space began to feel too small, and workers decided to look for an even larger location. In spite of their excellent track record, financial institutions were still unwilling to extend loans, primarily because of Rainbow's continuing ambiguous legal ownership status. After much discussion and legal consultation, Rainbow's workers voted in 1993 to legally become a worker-owned cooperative. Once Rainbow was owned by its workers, who were the sole shareholders, the banks could be more easily approached.

## Rainbow Moves to Its Current Folsom Street Location

The 1990s were reasonably good years for the Bay Area economy, and the public was interested in healthy food. Chains like Whole Foods catered to the growing public demand for convenience in addition to healthy food with attractive stores that had large parking lots, a delicatessen, and ready-to-eat specialty foods.

Despite the many challenges, Rainbow Cooperative decided to design and build a new state-of-the-art store at 13th and Folsom Streets. The new store, located in an "Enterprise Zone," was eligible for economic development funding. In return for promising to create jobs in the economically depressed community, Rainbow received a $1 million bank loan guaranteed by the City of San Francisco. The new building, owned by Rainbow Cooperative, opened its doors in 1996.

## Rainbow's Cooperative Structure

Once again, the move prompted a reorganization of Rainbow's business structure. In the new store, food and non-food items were on display

in a single area. The new structure divided the business into semi-in-
dependent departments that worked under the umbrella of the co-op.
Membership meetings, which included all workers, replaced the previous joint meetings between the grocery and general store workers.

Rainbow Grocery with worker-owner Josefa
Perez, 2015. Photo by Rezz Sacharoff.

Membership is the core of the business model and of the co-op's
functioning. New worker-members receive rigorous training that pre-
pares them for committee work and for exercising their vote at the
membership meetings. As co-op members, they also receive a share
of the annual surplus. At the membership meetings, worker-members
discuss issues that affect all of the workers and the co-op's overall operation. Since these meetings can involve a large number of members,
Rainbow has established guidelines for their smooth governance.

The co-op is divided into departments. Members work in semi-au-
tonomous sections that are responsible for a product line, such as grocery or bulk items, or in a non-product department, such as cashiering
or bookkeeping. Each department makes its own daily decisions regarding purchases and staffing.

The membership body as a whole elects a storewide steering committee, which meets weekly to address various departmental issues

and any conflicts that cannot be resolved within a department. The membership also elects a board of directors that focuses on long-term planning, development, finances, and legal issues.

The membership general assembly is the co-op's principal body. The role of membership in the overall business can be seen in the decisions taken—for example, the vote to discontinue the store's popular 20-percent-off coupon days. Many members felt that the discount days stretched the infrastructure of the business too thin by attracting huge crowds of shoppers. This added burden affected everything, from receiving and cashier lineups, through parking, to adequate product stocking.[9] Rainbow plans to replace the coupon days with a customer-appreciation discount program that will benefit frequent shoppers.

During the month of October, designated "National Co-op Month" by the co-op community, Rainbow sponsors onsite educational workshops where various Bay Area cooperators are invited to talk to shoppers about the benefits of cooperatives. These events are Rainbow's way of actively supporting the International Co-operative Alliance's principles of educating the public about cooperatives and supporting inter-co-op collaboration.

Democratic processes can be cumbersome for a large co-op like Rainbow, which currently employs more than 250 workers and serves an average of 3,000 customers a day. Membership meetings do not always come off without a hitch, but the co-op tries to resolve conflicts by using the tools developed over the years by its worker-members. For example, a trained Rainbow conflict resolution team and a civil rights advocacy committee exist to address individual grievances and conflicts and ensure a safe work environment that is free of harassment and discrimination.[10]

All workers are encouraged to formulate new ideas for replacing outdated tools and to propose new ways of complementing established traditions. The governing bodies within the business work hard to achieve the original goal of creating a harmonious workforce that is able to meet the daily demands of a large and growing business. A senior member attributes Rainbow's success to the balance it maintains between its unwavering commitment to its cooperative mission and the need for constant change, the ongoing rejuvenation of microstructures, and the development of new product lines to meet the needs of workers and the community.[11]

For their hard work, Rainbow workers are compensated with decent wages, as well as a share of the year-end patronage refund from the co-op's net surplus revenues. All workers receive full medical, dental, and vision plans, paid vacations, and generous discounts on purchases from Rainbow. Rainbow workers also receive a reciprocal discount at other Bay Area co-ops that participate in a co-op discount program. To top it all off, Rainbow workers are served hot organic, vegetarian meals at their worksite every day.

While recognizing its primary obligation to its workers, Rainbow also shares its surplus generously with schools and the community through a program of donations and grants. In addition, Rainbow extends an everyday discount to seniors, NoBAWC (Network of Bay Area Worker Cooperatives) members, and other community groups.[12] Rainbow supports other cooperatives and democratic workplaces by extending generous loans, sharing its knowledge, and supporting community-sponsored events. Rainbow's public-relations committee reaches out to the community with promotions and a variety of activities. In addition, Rainbow's specific business model has been used by other worker cooperatives to succeed in their own fields and communities.

In its daily operation, Rainbow ensures that knowledgeable workers are on the floor at all times and that all departments are well stocked. Customers get a quantity discount on unopened cases of groceries and sacks of bulk goods, as well as on supplements and other products purchased in volume; many people travel some distance every month to replenish their bulk pantries.[13] The store has a well-managed baked goods department and a well-stocked "grab and go" section, as well as carrying a wide range of food products to meet the diverse needs of vegetarians and vegans.

Rainbow is a staunch advocate of environmental awareness and energy efficiency. The co-op, in fact, exceeds the stringent standards necessary to be a certified San Francisco Green Business. In 2002, while replacing a leaky roof, Rainbow workers designed and installed three innovative green-energy projects, including daylight harvesting, solar electric arrays, and solar thermal panels. Rainbow's ecology committee educates the co-op's workers and shoppers about programs to reduce the environmental impact of their workplaces.

Recently, Rainbow has become even more proactive in providing local and seasonal food that has minimal ecological and social impact. The cheese, wine, and deli departments carry a variety of local products from small businesses, regional farms, and community artisans. Product selection has become increasingly challenging for health food markets, as consumers demand allergen-free, vegan, and gluten-free products, as well as products that are free of genetically modified organisms (GMO-free). Rainbow strongly supported California's Proposition 37, which would have required labeling of genetically modified foods. The co-op continues to educate its shoppers regarding GM foods, as well as about the legal issues small farmers and food-production businesses face.

With the organic and health food industry growing, all food co-ops, small and large, face challenges and competition. Rainbow is no exception. Health food chain stores have entered the market, buying up smaller businesses and using purely profit-motivated business practices, without regard for employee or community needs. As previously noted, in the face of rapidly rising rents, some of the longtime shoppers who support cooperative values have left San Francisco. Shoppers are also increasingly attracted to the chains by a combination of convenience and effective marketing. Much of the younger population lacks the time necessary to buy and prepare food, and this new clientele may not be aware of everything that goes on behind the scenes that distinguishes a co-op from a chain store.

> *"As a worker-owned cooperative, those of us who work here are more than simply the labor-force of this business, we are the business. . . . We all share the common desire to work in a non-hierarchical, democratic workplace where everyone's opinion matters. . . . Rainbow is more than just a job for us. And we hope that for you, our store is more than just a place to find healthy food."*[14]
> —A worker statement from Rainbow's website celebrating its fortieth anniversary in 2015

Today it is not enough for co-ops to match the choice, convenience, and affordability of chain stores. In a world where giant chains like Walmart and Costco carry organic food, the issue isn't just the products that co-ops sell but also how they sell them. Food co-ops must educate customers about cooperative values, including democratic governance and the political significance of people's product choices. Rainbow Grocery has demonstrated that this can be done effectively with active educational outreach programs and a strong ongoing dialogue with the community. Its connection to the community is what has kept Rainbow Cooperative growing and prospering.

## Notes

1.   "About," Rainbow Grocery, http://www.rainbow.coop/about/.
2.   "History of Rainbow Grocery: Part 1," a two-part history displayed on Rainbow's 2006 website. It was compiled by Tim Huet, a former Rainbow worker, who interviewed several of Rainbow's founding members to verify the details, and was edited by Rachel Forsmann.
3.   Ibid.
4.   People's Food System meeting notes, December 16, 1976. At this meeting participants were asked to "talk to Rainbow workers and straighten them out" regarding their alleged "uncooperative" attitudes.
5.   Author interview with Fred I, 2012. Fred is a longtime Rainbow worker.
6.   Arthur Lazere and Neil Bernstein, "Bumblebee Businesses: Members of the Briarpatch Network Practice Honest Business—and Make a Market Fly in 1988," *San Francisco Bay Guardian* 22, no. 28 (April 27, 1988): 14–18.
7.   Ibid., 17.
8.   Author conversation and e-mail communication with Mara Rivera, 2013. Mara worked at Rainbow in the 1980s.
9.   Author e-mail communication with Wind Jeff Drake, 2015. Wind Jeff is a Rainbow worker.
10.  Author interview with Jenny Glazer, 2012. Jenny was a longtime Rainbow worker.
11.  Author interview with Fred I, 2012. Fred is a longtime Rainbow worker.
12.  For an up-to-date list of groups that receive discounts at Rainbow, see www.rainbow.coop.
13.  For details about quantity discounts on various items and for updated discount flyers for different departments, see www.rainbow.coop.
14.  "About us," Rainbow Grocery, 2015, http://www.rainbow.coop/about-us/.

Much of the information on the history of Rainbow was obtained from Rainbow's old website dated 2006, www.rainbow.coop/aboutus/history, and from its current website in 2014. Information on Rainbow's structure was obtained from author interviews with Fred I and Jenny Glazer, two Rainbow workers, in 2010 and 2011, and from e-mail communication with Wind Jeff Drake, 2015.

# CHAPTER 5
# OTHER AVENUES FOOD
# STORE COOPERATIVE

NEAR THE WEST end of Golden Gate Park, just a few blocks from the Pacific Ocean, Other Avenues Food Cooperative offers fog and fresh air, along with healthy food. When a sunny day brings people to the ocean, they stop at Other Avenues for healthy snacks and organic fresh fruit and vegetables, but the majority of Other Avenues shoppers are local residents of the multiethnic Sunset and Richmond districts. Other Avenues strives to be a reliable, one-stop neighborhood natural food store, and a local resource for other environmentally friendly household products.

As its name implies, Other Avenues is a different kind of business. A new shopper may not be aware that no one person owns Other Avenues, but regular customers know how this community-centered business operates and support it partially because of its unique worker-owner structure.

OA, as Other Avenues is fondly known by its patrons, is one of the few food stores in the Bay Area that is totally committed to organic produce, groceries, and unpackaged bulk food items purchased from local farms and wholesalers.

Unlike other small businesses, Other Avenues is open 363 days a year, closed only on Dr. Martin Luther King Jr.'s birthday, to honor his life and legacy, and on May 1, International Workers Day, to celebrate the rights of workers all over the world.

## The Birth of Other Avenues with the Support of the People's Food System

OA was established in the mid-1970s by a group of volunteers from the community who were part of the San Francisco Bay Area Food

Other Avenues logo, 2015. Photo by Rezz Sacharoff.

Conspiracy, which eventually gave rise to the People's Food System and a handful of retail stores, the first among them being Seeds of Life in the Mission District, the Noe Valley Community Store, and Other Avenues on Judah Street near 46th Avenue in the Outer Sunset District, two blocks from its current site.

In the 1970s, small businesses could afford to rent in San Francisco, and there were other progressive businesses in the Outer Sunset area, including an independent movie theatre, a café, and a community dance studio that served the neighborhood on a shoestring budget. The quiet neighborhood by the sea, where everyone knew each other, their children, and their dogs, provided a loyal customer base.

Other Avenues opened its doors in 1974 with a small grant from the People's Food System and some fundraising efforts by community members. OA's first location kept irregular business hours and was run by a constantly changing, largely volunteer staff. During those years, while other PFS stores were thriving, Other Avenues could barely keep its doors open. The business aspect of the co-op was treated informally, and in many ways OA was still operating like a food-buying club, in that there was no distinction between the shoppers and the workers who were ringing up the food. A small margin on the cost of food paid the rent and utilities. It was only when a group of committed workers and shoppers decided to turn the store into a stable community market that it started to take shape as a business.

> *"It was not unusual to read a sign that said, 'The store is closed because today's volunteer did not show up.'"*[1]
> —Judy Watson, volunteer
> from late 1970 to 2007

All these years later, Other Avenues has become a successful worker-owned cooperative. Other Avenues is not just a health food store; it is a welcoming community center where shoppers not only buy food, but also socialize, attend educational workshops, and share their lives.

## By Any Other Name

There are many theories about the origin of the name Other Avenues. One story has it that in the revolutionary 1960s a group of street journalists in the East Village in New York City started a paper called the *East Village Other* as an alternative to *The Village Voice*, which they felt had become too mainstream. Small businesses with names like "The Other Place," "The Other Boutique," and "The Other Restaurant" soon appeared in the Village. This "Other" wave subsequently traveled to San Francisco. There was a café named "The Other Café" in the Inner Sunset District of the city. Some say that the pioneers of Other Avenues Food Store used the term to convey the fact that, located in "The Avenues" of San Francisco, the store was an alternative to a conventional market, hence the name "Other Avenues."

## Challenging Years

During its early volunteer-run days, OA's weekly meetings to address various community issues were open to workers and shoppers alike. Decisions were made by consensus, a model adopted from the Food Conspiracy and still used today for most of OA's business meetings.

Once the volunteers decided to hire two paid workers to regularly staff the store and to ensure more consistent business hours, OA began to attract even more shoppers. Although management was still minimal, and the store was not particularly profitable, the low rent allowed the store to remain open.

OA's isolated location posed a challenge. As the internal conflicts within the People's Food System worsened, it became increasingly difficult for OA to purchase food, particularly fresh produce, without a dedicated store vehicle. Although the close-knit neighborhood supported the store in any way it could, its loyal base was simply too small. At that time, there was very little commerce at the far end of the N-Judah streetcar line, and there was not much foot traffic in the area. Vendors complained about having to come so far for small deliveries.

By the end of the 1970s, Other Avenues was on the brink of closure. With only a flicker of hope remaining, a series of fundraising events organized by community members—including a garage sale, a bake sale, and a concert—paid the rent and purchased an old truck. Two workers began to pick up fresh produce daily from the Alemany Farmers Market.[2] With the reliable supply, sales increased, and after a few months, the store was able to buy basic equipment, including scales and a cash register.

By 1980, the small store carried a good inventory of fresh produce and cheese, as well as a few other bulk food items. Seeing the fresh produce, including ethnic items, arriving every day encouraged many Middle Eastern immigrants living in the neighborhood to begin shopping regularly at OA. Early in the morning, a group of Arab women frequently gathered outside of the store before it opened, singing in anticipation of fresh fruits and vegetables.

In 1982, after two years of economic surplus, Other Avenues moved to its current location, a double storefront at 3930 Judah Street. Given that OA had no fixed business structure, this was a big step. The store hired more staff, but when sales didn't increase, it began to lose money. It was small loans from community members and from the Cheese Board Collective in Berkeley that kept the shelves full for a while, allowing the new location to begin to attract more shoppers and volunteers.

Eventually, the store was divided into departments to facilitate better management, and, with advice from community members with business skills, the workers began to improve their decision-making process. Despite the negative cash flow, spirits remained high, and workers and volunteers, who felt they were making positive economic and political contributions to the neighborhood, believed they could survive and succeed. Even the workers' children felt a sense of belonging to the co-op community. Their enthusiasm was reflected in the games they played outside on the sidewalk.

> *"Our children, Sonia and Serena, were role-playing as OA's produce buyers Carol & Shelly. How wonderful [it was] that they were emulating real life heroes and not playing Barbies."*[3]
> —Alice Tilson (Sonia's mother), an OA shopper and community member

By 1984, in spite of the consistent enthusiasm of customers and staff, OA's financial situation was deteriorating. Then, an internal struggle later called "the war of the '80s" arose among the workers. The staff was divided into two factions: those who wanted long-term structured democratic governance, and those who resisted "becoming a business." Meetings were bitter, which adversely affected the business. Community members with arbitration skills intervened when they saw that the co-op was in danger of closing. They assisted with the meetings and drafted solutions that both parties could accept. Some workers left at that point, but those who felt confident about the future of Other Avenues stayed on.

In 1987, with the help of two Berkeley business consultants, OA was structured as a "hybrid consumer co-op," governed by a board of directors that was composed of workers and consumers from the community.[4] Although, at that time, OA did not officially incorporate as a co-op, the workers met weekly to discuss the management of daily operations, and the board met monthly to discuss overall financial and community matters. To reward shoppers' loyalty and to involve the community, OA offered shoppers the opportunity to purchase membership cards that entitled them to a discount on groceries and a vote at board elections.

Despite the workers' determination, an accountant offered a very pessimistic assessment of OA's financial feasibility. He advised the workers to close the store, but they refused. They began an aggressive membership drive, setting up tables outside the store every weekend and urging customers to buy the discount card. The store began to carry more organic food, and, with a modest loan from shoppers, the produce and bulk food sections were expanded. In spite of these efforts, poor sales forced the store to reduce its staff of fifteen to five dedicated workers, all of whom accepted substantial salary cuts in the hope of keeping the store open.

> *"The accountant looked at OA's books and told the workers, 'What you really need to do is put a lock on the front door and walk away!'"*[5]
> —Consultant Bob Gould in conversation with Steve Bosserman, a former worker at Other Avenues

Despite the financial turbulence, OA continued to connect with the neighborhood. The store brought people in to offer educational classes on subjects such as how to compost food scraps and how to cook nutritious vegetarian meals. OA also sponsored educational lectures on how to participate in food safety standard initiatives. The workers maintained an alliance with the food and justice community at large. They regularly donated food to Food Not Bombs, a community kitchen offering free food. In 1988, when the United Farm Workers Union called for a third boycott of table grapes because hazardous pesticides were harming farmworkers' health, OA honored the boycott, despite the fact that nearby competing stores continued to carry the grapes.

In the midst of this financial hardship, a Sunset community member with an accounting background stepped in, becoming OA's financial consultant for more than a decade.[6] She explained to workers about how to interpret financial documents, and she helped them improve OA's governance structure. She chaired the weekly business meetings and later taught the workers how to structure their meetings. She also helped the workers form committees to carry out necessary research. This hands-on consultation helped to transform Other Avenues from a struggling co-op into a stable business with a vision for the future. As it regained its morale, OA attracted more volunteers to help with labor and sales. Outstanding bills were paid, and new workers were hired. The next few years were financially tough but promising.

Demonstration to "Save Organic Standards," 1997. Other Avenues worker-owners: Shanta Sacharoff, Tina Rodia, Barb Reusch, and Colin Coyne as well as Shanta's daughter Serena (not a worker-owner). Photo courtesy of the author.

## Stability with Community Involvement

As sales improved, OA was able to expand its role in the community and to support the other PFS survivors. The co-op participated in local community events and neighborhood festivals and broadened its outreach program of classes and workshops. In 1994, OA joined Rainbow, the Inner Sunset Community Store, the Noe Valley Community Store, and Veritable Vegetable to create an umbrella organization called the Inter-collective Organic Union to expand consumer awareness about ecological food issues, including local and organic farming, and to educate the public about the benefits of supporting cooperatives.

Other Avenues had an active volunteer labor pool from its inception, but the program had been fairly disorganized. Members of the community signed up to contribute time to running the store in exchange for a discount on their groceries. In the mid-1990s, a worker with the necessary skills stepped in to better organize the program, training and scheduling volunteers to work in the departments that needed them, making the program an integral part of the store's business plan. Volunteers reduced labor costs and took a strong interest in OA's success.

# Intercollective Organic Union

1899 Mission St.
@ 15th St.
863-0620
Mon-Sat 9:00 am - 8:30 pm
Sun 10:00 am - 8:30 pm

1599 Sanchez St.
@ 29th St.
824-8022
Mon-Sat. 8:30 am - 8:00 pm
Sundays 9:00 am - 4:00 pm

**INNER SUNSET COMMUNITY FOOD STORE**

1319 20th Ave. @ Irving
664-5363
10:00 am - 8:00 pm daily

**Other Avenues**
A co-op and a collective
3930 Judah St. @ 44th Ave.
10 - 8 daily          661-7475

Flyer created to unite the surviving four store fronts, 1992. Created by Donald Francis, Carlo Denefeld, Debbie Benrubi, and Shanta Sacharoff.

At this time, the Inner Sunset Community Store, located only twenty-four blocks away from OA, was facing irresolvable difficulties and, in 1995, it folded. This left OA the only natural food co-op serving the west side of the city.

These were also good years for Other Avenues in a number of other ways. Public interest in healthy food had increased, and new Sunset District residents had more money to spend. OA responded to this demand with a better-trained staff and a dedicated business consultant, who taught workers crucial business skills.

By 1995, OA had paid off its outstanding debts and was able to buy new equipment and expand its inventory. OA's improved stability meant that suppliers were willing to provide goods on more financially favorable terms, improving OA's cash flow. A long-time PFS produce supplier, Veritable Vegetable, began to deliver produce regularly, allowing OA to get rid of its costly delivery truck. The renewed relationship with VV definitely helped OA make its produce department more profitable.

In the late 1990s, OA took a bold step, making the entire produce department organic. This meant that less expensive commercial produce was no longer sold at OA, and some popular items were no longer stocked, if no organic option was available. Some shoppers were disgruntled at first, but as organic produce grew more popular, and organic farms gained more market support, fresh staples were usually well stocked. Soon, shoppers were saying how happy they were to be able to shop in a produce department where they didn't have to watch out for non-organic items.

Many natural food markets began having deli sections to serve community members looking for healthy ready-to-eat food. OA developed its "OA's Own" (pronounced "O-A zone") products, a line of unique fresh food made on the store's premises. These original and popular products now include OA's Own salsa, tahuna (vegan "tuna" pâté), and raw "donut holes."

OA has always been involved in food activism, and in 1997, when the USDA proposed a bill to dilute organic food standards by permitting methods such as irradiation and the use of sewage sludge as fertilizer and certifying genetically modified items as organic, OA's workers and shoppers joined with other consumers and organic growers to protest this proposition and to "Save Organic Standards." After receiving more than 275,000 comments from the public opposing the proposal, the Department of Agriculture backed down.

On another occasion, Starbucks wanted to open a coffee shop near Other Avenues. OA workers and volunteers gathered more than four thousand signatures and held rallies opposing the venture, convincing the San Francisco Planning Commission to rule against the chain opening a store in the residential neighborhood. In its place, an independent small business, an organic juice bar, Judahlicious, does a booming business.

In return, the community has shown its commitment to supporting Other Avenues. In the late 1990s, workers and shoppers felt threatened when the building that houses OA was put up for sale. A community member and volunteer stepped in and purchased the building, preventing an unreasonable rent increase and allowing OA to remain in its location.[7] It seemed that finally, after years of struggle, OA was financially and materially stable.

## The Making of a Successful Worker-Owned and Community-Centered Cooperative

As the workers began to operate the business more effectively, community board members started to defer to them when making business decisions. It was around this time that the workers began to discuss applying for worker-owned cooperative status. At the October 1998 annual meeting, the members voted to restructure OA, and in 1999, OA legally incorporated as a worker-owned cooperative.

The store began to broaden its customer base and increase revenues, and product variety increased in step. With an improved cash flow and a new supplements buyer, OA expanded its vitamin department in 2002. At the same time, with the help of a major supplier, the bulk food section was reorganized and enlarged. This section would later earn OA *San Francisco Weekly*'s award for the "Best Bulk Food Store."[8]

## The End of the Volunteer Program

OA was founded by volunteers, and the workers' strong commitment to a vibrant volunteer program continued even after OA became worker-owned. Volunteers, who took a strong interest in the store, provided not only labor, but also a loyal customer base that bridged the gap between shoppers and workers. Some offered informal advice, while others served on the board. Some provided educational workshops, and others helped with backyard gardening. In return, OA offered them a substantial discount on groceries and a friendly atmosphere for socializing and learning about healthy food.

It was during this period of stability that Other Avenues found out that more and more co-ops were discontinuing their volunteer programs for labor and tax-related reasons. In addition to fears about the potential legal ramifications, many OA workers felt that the business needed the stability provided by paid labor, rather than continuing to rely on unpaid volunteers. In 2007, the worker-owners decided to end the store's beloved volunteer program. Many volunteers, particularly those who had worked for the store for decades, were very upset, and workers responded by promising the co-op would increase its outreach programs in order to strengthen the store's relationship with the community.

> *"This [the end of the volunteer program]*
> *was indeed a very gloomy day for*
> *both the volunteers and the workers.*
> *Truly, it was an end of a community/*
> *cooperative era! Many volunteers who*
> *had cared for OA for a long time felt*
> *abandoned, disappointed, and angry."[9]*
> —The author's sentiment
> regarding the end of the volunteer
> program at Other Avenues

## Other Avenues Buys Its Building

The Other Avenues building was again up for sale in March 2008, and this time the workers decided to buy the building themselves to secure the store's location of twenty-eight years. In the midst of the financial uncertainty of the mortgage industry meltdown, what bank would extend a mortgage to a worker-owned co-op? Community members, other co-ops, such as Rainbow Grocery, the Cheese Board, Arizmendi Bakery, and Veritable Vegetable, and some worker-owners loaned money for the down payment, an expression of their commitment to sustaining the co-op.

> *"While daunting, we saw the challenge*
> *and responsibility as being the best*
> *possible business decision. . . . We entered*
> *a new phase of business ownership*
> *partnered with property ownership."[10]*
> —Tina Rodia, a longtime
> OA worker-owner

A business plan was constructed that looked favorable enough to assure a local bank that the store could make mortgage payments and repay loans. In retrospect, the timing was right; a few months later the American real estate market collapsed, and bank mortgages became even harder to obtain. OA has now refinanced the mortgage and paid off the community loans.

Other Avenues, 2015. Photo by Rezz Sacharoff.

## Other Avenues Now

Worker ownership has been empowering at OA and has created a new sense of responsibility among the workers. Once hired, every prospective worker-owner receives rigorous training, allowing both the co-op and the applicant the opportunity to determine their mutual compatibility. When necessary, the applicant's training period is extended. Occasionally, the co-op has to let an applicant who proves unsuitable go. After the trial period, the applicant is voted in as a worker-owner. Workers receive medical insurance, a generous discount on groceries, and other benefits. On an annual basis, after all expenses have been paid and a reserve has been set aside, the worker-owners share any remaining surplus based on their labor contribution that year.

Operationally, Other Avenues is divided into product line departments—packaged foods, produce, housewares, etc.—that are staffed and managed by the workers, with most workers working in more than one department. In addition, all workers are expected to do routine daily work, such as cashiering, customer service, administrative tasks, and maintenance work. Duties are shared as much as possible, with work and shifts occasionally rotated to maintain the co-op's egalitarian structure while building new leadership.

## Governance Structure

For legal purposes, three officers—the president, the secretary, and the chief financial officer—are elected annually at an OA board meeting. However, once elected as a member, a worker is automatically a board member and shares in all decision-making. Thus, OA is run by direct rather than representative democracy. At Other Avenues board meetings, the goal is not a majority vote, but a group consensus that everyone can work with. Outside of board meetings, committees conduct research necessary to facilitate decision-making. Knowing that everyone's voice is heard, most workers feel empowered both individually and as a group. Nonetheless, OA's bylaws allow its board to use a majority vote to resolve legal issues and address challenges that threaten to become roadblocks.

> *"OA's size makes it possible to use direct democracy in its governance. And, to me, it is the major benefit of being a worker-member here."[11]*
> —Angelynne Burke, a longtime previous OA worker

Even in a small group, the collective process can be challenging, particularly when opinions clash. On occasion, a major business decision can be made quickly—like a dream! Other times, a sensitive issue requires laborious discussion, making it a nightmare. Trained professionals who are familiar with cooperative governance can help to unravel unresolved issues and put them on the table, allowing the group to move forward. In both 2014 and 2015, OA's staff had to bring in outside professionals to arbitrate issues that the workers were unable to resolve on their own.

Workers take turns making lunch for everyone on board meeting days. This allows OA workers to nurture one another and to sample a variety of cuisines. Sharing food boosts morale, reminds workers of their collective roots, and sets a positive tone for productive meetings. Below is an example of one of the OA workers' favorite lunch entrées. The many vegetables available on the premises help make this is an inexpensive and nutritious dish.

## ☺Worker Lunch Favorite☺
### Sāmbhar: A South Indian Soup (A Meal in a Pot)

*Sāmbhar* is a type of *dal* or soup made with split beans or lentils. Dal (also spelled *dahl* or *daal*) is a typical entrée to accompany any Indian meal. The consistency of a dal can vary depending on other items on the menu. Here the hearty sāmbhar is made with a variety of vegetables.

The important last step in making the soup is *vaghar* or tempering. The vaghar sets the dal apart from any other soup.

- 8 cups water
- 1 cup red lentils, rinsed and drained thoroughly
- 1 teaspoon salt
- 1 fresh hot green chili, such as jalapeno, minced after core and seeds are removed
- 1 tablespoon grated fresh ginger root
- ½ teaspoon each: ground coriander and turmeric
- 1 tablespoon safflower, canola, or olive oil
- ¼ cup onion, finely chopped
- ¼ cup bell pepper (any color), finely chopped
- 1 cup cauliflower or broccoli, florets only, cut small
- 1 cup each: carrot, eggplant, celery, zucchini, and tomatoes, cut into ¼-inch cubes
- 1 tablespoon shredded dried coconut
- A few sprigs of fresh cilantro
- 2–3 tablespoons of freshly squeezed lime juice
- For *vaghar*:
- 1 tablespoon cooking oil
- 1 teaspoon black or brown mustard seeds
- ½ teaspoon cumin seeds
- 2 or 3 whole dried hot red chilis
- A pinch of hing (asafetida), optional (available at Indian grocery stores and at Other Avenues)

In a large soup pot, bring the water to a boil and add the drained lentils. Simmer briskly uncovered for 15 minutes. Add the salt, green chili, ginger, coriander, and turmeric. Cover and simmer for 20 minutes more over a moderate heat.

Heat the oil in a frying pan and sauté the onions and peppers for a few minutes. Add the chopped vegetables and shredded coconut and stir-fry together for 5 minutes. Add vegetable mixture and the lime juice to the pot. Turn down the heat and continue to simmer the soup.

When making the vaghar, keep the cover for the cooking pot close at hand. In a small saucepan, or a metal measuring cup, heat the oil. Add the mustard seeds. When they start to pop, add the cumin seeds and dry red chilis. Then, moving quickly, add the optional hing, stir and then pour this smoky oil mixture into the pot of dal. You can dip the small pan or measuring cup right into the dal to get all of the spice mixture into the pot quickly. Cover immediately. Turn off the heat, and keep the pot covered for 5 minutes. Uncover, stir, correct the seasoning, and garnish with cilantro. Instruct your diners to remove the whole red chili pieces from the sāmbhar before they eat it.

Makes 8 to 10 servings

Recipe adapted from *Flavors of India* by Shanta Nimbark Sacharoff.[12]

## Bringing It Back to the Community

Currently, Other Avenues cooperative is a flourishing business that employs twenty worker-owners and serves 500 to 600 customers daily. The gross revenue for 2014 was $4 million. As sales increased and the customer base grew broader, the product line selection also expanded. The demand for healthy food is currently growing. The all-organic produce department remains the store's biggest draw, and the eco-friendly bulk foods, packaged groceries, and supplements departments continue to grow. The OA's Own organic and raw deli is a favorite among the regulars, who can now enjoy their food at the parklet that was built in front of the store. More cruelty-free body products and fair-trade items, as well as books by local authors, fill up the shelves, as do the growing number of green cleaning products and appliances. The busy wine and beer departments carry both imported and local products.

Not all of OA's workers are vegetarians, and the co-op gets frequent requests for organic and grass-fed meat products. Whether or not to carry meat is an ongoing debate, but for now the co-op continues its established practice of providing the community with plant-based foods.

Clearly, without the support of the surrounding community, loyal customers, other cooperatives, reliable suppliers, and the farming community, OA would not be the successful business it is today, and Other Avenues reciprocates in any way it can. Customer service is extremely important at Other Avenues. Frequent shoppers are encouraged to purchase a Red Discount Card that entitles them to a store discount. This arrangement benefits both the shoppers, who save on groceries, and the co-op, which gains steady customers. Seniors, members of the Bicycle Coalition and the San Francisco Vegetarian Society, workers from other Bay Area worker cooperatives, and workers in the nearby neighborhood businesses do not have to buy a discount card to receive discounts on their groceries at OA. As well, other programs and initiatives are established as the co-op's year-end surplus permits.

> "Other Avenues embodies the progressive values and health-consciousness that give the neighborhood of Judah Beach its character. . . . They're the pioneers."[13]
> —San Francisco Bay Guardian on Other Avenues receiving the Best Co-op Award at its 2005 Small Business Awards

Besides the various discounts, Other Avenues annually reserves approximately 20 percent of its gross surplus to support a variety of community causes, including giving discounts to neighboring schools through a scrip purchasing program, giving donations to fundraising events for nonprofits, sponsoring cultural venues throughout the city, and attending and sponsoring educational workshops and community events. Two events that receive regular support are the Sunset Community Festival and the World Vegetarian Weekend, sponsored by the San Francisco Vegetarian Society. OA has received several distinguished awards from local newspapers and government agencies in recognition of its dedication to the community.

In return, the community has always assisted the co-op with necessary projects. In 2015, the community helped Other Avenues raise

more than its $48,000 to install the long-awaited solar panels neces-
sary to reduce the co-op's energy bills and to advance its green business plans.

OA connects with other cooperatives in the Bay Area by supporting and participating in many of the events sponsored by other organizations, including the California Center for Cooperative Development
(CCCD), an educational institute that supports the cooperative movement in the Bay Area and throughout the state; the United States
Federation of Worker Cooperatives (USFWC), a national umbrella organization that unites worker-owned cooperatives throughout
the nation; and the local Network of Bay Area Worker Cooperatives
(NoBAWC), which is dedicated to the advancement of workplace democracy in the San Francisco Bay Area.

To maintain the values of the People's Food System, Other Avenues
continues to support organic farmers and sustainable business practices and to advance community building by actively reaching out to
local small businesses, co-op suppliers, and fair-trade vendors, as well
as maintaining a strong, egalitarian structure of governance.

> *"Our once-fringe fantasies of*
> *cooperation and egalitarianism*
> *within the workplace may someday*
> *be considered the new normal"*[14]
> —Nicole Gluckstern, a former
> employee at Other Avenues

The United Nations designated 2012 as the International Year of
Cooperatives (IYC) to recognize socio-economic advantages cooperatives provide to the world's communities. Cooperatives and their allies
held events to raise public awareness of the cooperative movement in
the Bay Area. Bay Area food co-ops asked their local governments and
global activist leaders to support growth and stability for cooperatives
and to address food sovereignty issues. For its part, Other Avenues
celebrated IYC by offering its customers additional discounts and organizing special educational events focusing on the importance of cooperatives to our shopper community.

This sort of mutually beneficial relationship is the source of
OA's continuing stability. In 2014 Other Avenues and its community

proudly celebrated OA's fortieth anniversary and its enduring mission: Healthy Community, Healthy Planet, and Healthy Business!

## Notes

1.  Judy Watson volunteered at the co-op for more than three decades. Judy's mother, Lucy, was one of the founding members of Other Avenues.
2.  The two volunteers Other Avenues hired were Stanley Sacharoff and Jim Sugarek. Their dedication and the daily fresh produce delivery allowed Other Avenues to generate its first surplus.
3.  Alice Tilson was a member of the community who regularly shopped at Other Avenues.
4.  The two consultants Other Avenues hired were Jaques Kaswan and Pete Lee. They were instrumental in planting the seeds for the co-op's future worker-owner structure.
5.  Stephen Bosserman, "OA Memories," *Other Ave-News*, Fall 1999.
6.  The community member in question is Anne Ackerman, who was given the title "Mother of OA." Anne worked as OA's financial consultant for more than fifteen years. Along with her husband Robert Vernick, she also volunteered in the co-op's cheese department for many years. Like Anne, many community volunteers helped to build both OA's business and community.
7.  Ralph Lane, who volunteered at Other Avenues for many years, bought the building in 1998 to secure Other Avenues' location.
8.  *San Francisco Weekly*, May 28, 2008, http://www.sfweekly.com/sanfrancisco/best-bulk-food-store/BestOf?oid=2203947.
9.  Author's personal observation as someone who worked closely with many of these volunteers.
10. Tina Rodia, "What's New?" *Other Ave-News*, April 2008. Tina was an Other Avenues worker-owner from 2000 to 2015.
11. Angelynne Burke worked at Other Avenues for more than two decades.
12. Modified from: Shanta Nimbark Sacharoff, *Flavors of India* (San Francisco: 101 Productions, 1980).
13. *San Francisco Bay Guardian*, April 27, 2005, http://www.sfbg.com, gave Other Avenues the "Best Co-op Award" at the newspaper's 2005 Small Business Awards.
14. Nicole Gluckstern, "Part Three: The Future," *Other Ave-News*, Spring 2015, 1–2. This was part of a three-part series entitled "Other Avenues Celebrates 40 Years." Nicole was an Other Avenues worker-owner from 2007 to 2015.

# PART III
# FOOD SHARING BUILDS COMMUNITY

HUMAN CIVILIZATION HAS been shaped and defined by food growing, food gathering, food festivities, and everyday food sharing. Food brings us together when we cultivate and harvest it, and when we shop for it, prepare it, and share it. Many of our most powerful traditions have grown up around food sharing; surely one cannot underestimate the importance of food sharing in shaping our lives.

Industrialization has had a tremendous impact on longstanding food-sharing customs and ceremonies. Our working life has shifted from a largely agricultural collaborative exchange tied to the land, the seasons, and food to dehumanized, competitive assembly-line work based on efficiency and profit-making. As the industrial economy demands that people work like machines chained to their work posts, average consumers have little time to enjoy and share food that is the fruit of their own labor. Eating food has transitioned from a community ritual to a form of commodified consumption. For many, food has become merely a biological necessity that takes up too much of their apparently scarce time.

In the 1970s, The Bay Area's People's Food System was one group among many to address our dehumanized relationship with food and its distribution. Along with other food activists and farmers, the San Francisco Bay Area's People's Food System sought to bring healthy food to the people.

Today there is a growing movement among many of the world's people decrying and challenging the deterioration of the link between food and culture and seeking to bring the sacred gift of food sharing back to modern civilization. Farmers, consumers, progressive chefs, and homemakers are working together to produce and use food in ways that are environmentally sustainable and once again make food culturally nourishing and enjoyable.

# CHAPTER 6
# MY JOURNEY WITH BAY AREA FOOD
# CO-OPS AND OTHER AVENUES

I CAME FROM India to New York, and then, in 1970, from New York to San Francisco. I connected with the early food-sharing clubs, which evolved into a group of work collectives known as the People's Food System. I later helped to establish Other Avenues, one of the surviving co-ops of that era. I have long been politically, socially, and personally motivated by a desire to rediscover and nourish the lost link between food and community. I have seen the power of food sharing in its many forms, bringing people together and reminding us that we are deeply connected to one another and to the earth. I continue to cultivate, teach, collaborate, and encourage food sharing. This chapter is my story.

## Where Do I Fit?
When I arrived in the Bay Area, people on the street were talking about organizing and sharing food, homes, work, and family. Coming from the Big Apple, I was surprised to see how trusting people were here! It was a time of solidarity in opposition to the dehumanization of corporate growth and a war machine that was increasingly out of touch with the people.

I was raised by a vegetarian Hindu family in Gujarat, a northwestern state in India. In my village, sharing fresh food with others was the way of our life. Everyone worked in the fields and everyone ate. My father was the temple keeper. Local farmers always gifted new crops to the gods, and my family was allowed to keep this food as *Prasad*, which means "God's leftovers." My mother always prepared extra food in anticipation of the hungry traveler who might be stopping at the temple. She was a wonderful cook, and village folks used to say that she could create food out of dirt. (This was particularly true once when a bowl of mung beans gifted to the temple contained more pebbles than beans.) Although the village was not prosperous, the community was oriented around food production, and we shared what food we had, so there were no beggars. Our food sharing extended to the gods, and even to stray dogs.

When I came to New York to study, I missed this relationship to food and community intensely. I was disappointed that there was no fresh food available at the college. Later, when I moved to San Francisco, I found all kinds of fresh foods year-round, and I was happy to see so many people engaged in the communal activities of selecting, cooking, and sharing food.

In San Francisco, I found produce markets that sold colorful fresh fruits and vegetables to people of many cultures. Small health food stores and ethnic markets owned by immigrant families carried a variety of vegetables that were difficult to find at supermarkets. Like the food bazaars of India, these stores sold bulk food out of big burlap bags, boxes, and baskets. I could touch and smell the food and verify its freshness. Every weekend, there was a large farmers market on Alemany Boulevard with all kinds of fruits and vegetables, including many varieties unique to Mexican cooking and other ethnic cuisines. This is commonplace now, but, at the time, coming from New York, it was new and unique for me.

Ethnic food stores and farmers markets became my new libraries. I visited them all and learned about items that were unfamiliar to me by talking to the people who bought them. Many free carnivals and food festivals focused on uniting particular groups or bringing people together around political issues. Those of us who were working on food and justice issues learned from one another how to organize community activities at a street level.

I made many new friends at these shops and street fairs. We shared recipes, food-related experiences, information, and activities. We told one another about restaurants that were inexpensive and authentic. We organized cooking classes to share our various native cuisines, and initiated food-sharing projects to bring our families and neighbors together.

It did not take me long to find an interesting group of people who were organizing food-buying clubs they called the Food Conspiracy.

Using a democratic management method that they had devised themselves, Food Conspiracy members gathered to buy healthy food in bulk and then divide it among themselves. They bought fresh produce and dry goods in large quantities from wholesalers, making the food more affordable than in retail health food stores. Sharing in the work of buying and dividing the food was both a fun community activity and a politically galvanizing action. The Food Conspiracy soon expanded into a network of groups that actively supported one another. It seemed to me like a small village building a community around food. I felt right at home!

## Food Sharing

In addition to sharing the work of communally buying and dividing up the food, Food Conspiracy members organized social gatherings and food-related events. On the weekly food-ordering day, everyone brought food to share with our neighborhood Haight-Ashbury Food Conspiracy. Over potluck dinners we—women from many cultures— identified community needs and organized political actions in the neighborhood.

We discussed the problem of growing world hunger and what we could do to help, while building our own community. Not all Food Conspiracy members were vegetarian, but we only brought vegetarian dishes to share, and this practice became the status quo for our potlucks. We were familiar with Frances Moore Lappé's *Diet for a Small Planet,* which described how a plant-centered diet could help solve world hunger, and we were all willing participants in the meatless revolution.[1]

We learned about food and nutrition and taught one another what we learned. Some Food Conspiracy members conducted food- and nutrition-related research, for example, determining which herbs and spices had health benefits and what vegetarian protein alternatives were adequate substitutes for meat, particularly for children. A rotating list of individuals led these discussions, so that everyone had the opportunity to learn and share as much as possible. These clubs were specifically women-centered cottage industries, with no elected officers or leadership positions.

Although I didn't know many people, I was always cooking and sharing meals with a few friends and their companions. I was pregnant then for the first time, and it just seemed to be a natural maternal instinct. Sharing food was also a great social resource. I was learning how to cook with ingredients from various ethnic cuisines. Trying new recipes and creating my own was a newly acquired passion. I grew up as the youngest child in my family, and, unlike most Indian girls, I had no interest in cooking. I told my mother that I was not going to get married, so I wouldn't have to learn to cook. Little did I know that later in life I would have to acquire this skill to sustain my vegetarian diet in the United States, and that cooking and sharing food would become very important to me. I wanted to recreate my family recipes and share them with others. When I wrote home to my sisters requesting recipes and cooking tips, they were truly surprised!

Nimbark sisters cooking for an event, 1999. Photo by Rick Sugarek.

The collective household I lived in further enhanced my interest in preparing and sharing food. Other people living in the house also wanted to acquire and share culinary knowledge. At that time, in San Francisco, there were many collective households of like-minded people. Our group had five members, and we shared all housekeeping chores, including cooking and cleaning. Members of the household asked me to teach cooking classes once a week, and these classes became regular food-sharing parties. Participants asked questions about spices and other ingredients. I was shocked to discover how many people were unfamiliar with the delights and possibilities of the spices that I had grown up with, so I organized a tour of specialty stores to acquaint people with the great variety of spices and ethnic food ingredients available in the Bay Area.

Other people were eager to share their cooking skills and traditions, and the cooking classes rapidly expanded. I taught people how to teach cooking using my hands-on methods and learned to cook ethnic dishes from others. A participant in my classes encouraged me to write a vegetarian Indian cookbook.[2] At first, I felt that the task of writing a book was beyond me, but it soon proved to be the perfect work for me while I was caring for my newborn son. I created new recipes and polished up old ones, establishing specific measurements and holding taste testings. There were always many eager Food Conspiracy guinea pigs!

I had trouble finding a publisher who was willing to publish a vegetarian cookbook. Even in the progressive Bay Area of the 1970s, publishers thought that no one would buy an Indian cookbook that did not include meat recipes. Little did they know that the Bay Area's food politics were ready and the audience hungry for the many ethnic vegetarian cookbooks that would be published in the next decade. I finally found a small publishing house that produced only cookbooks; mine would be their second vegetarian cookbook. *Flavors of India* was published soon after my son, Reyaz, took his first steps in 1972. The book has since been reprinted numerous times and continues to sell steadily to this day.[3]

When Food Conspiracy food-buying clubs grew too big to handle, we gathered to discuss the possibility of opening food stores to better manage food distribution and to serve more people. Our goal was to continue to distribute "Food for People, Not for Profit." At that time, some of us, particularly the women, were concerned that the proposed new system of stores would diminish the empowerment we had gained in the Food Conspiracy. Food Conspiracy meetings were cultural gatherings, whereas a series of stores sounded too much like a business. Nonetheless, we were all excited by the prospect of expansion. It took a great many fundraisers to open the Haight Community Food Store, where I first learned about volunteering.

At the time, there was also a resurgence of interest in Asian philosophy; everything Indian was considered exotic and wonderful. I began to regularly teach Indian cooking classes to small groups in my home. The success of *Flavors of India* helped me to advertise my

Collaborative ad taken from *San Francisco Bay Guardian*, 1994. Courtesy of the author's archive.

classes in local newspapers. Soon, I had a regular flow of students and a new source of income. Students would cook with me, share the meals we had prepared, and take the recipes home.

During the period of the mid-1970s when a section of the leadership of the People's Food System increasingly focused on a bigger revolutionary picture, most of the women I worked with maintained a more grassroots support network. For us, the personal remained political; our network consisted of child-care co-ops, home-study classes, and women's groups. Food distribution and food sharing was the thread that held us together.

## Other Avenues Food Co-op

When I moved to the Outer Sunset District, a few blocks away from the Pacific Ocean, there was a collectively run food store in my neighborhood called Other Avenues (OA). I started to volunteer at OA in the produce department. Starting the day with the smell of colorful fresh fruits and vegetables was the best part of the task, and feeling the ocean air in the morning was refreshing.

At the time, OA had just moved from a tiny space into a much larger two-door market. In the new space the shelves were largely empty, and the volunteer workers were at a loss as to how to bring in new customers. There was very little structured staffing or shifts. We started to organize ourselves, developing a fixed rotation of workers who purchased fresh produce and others who opened and closed the store. My first job was to stock and arrange the fresh greens. Later, as the department grew, I trained other volunteers.

After several months, I began to offer freshly prepared foods, including sandwiches, chutney, and salsa, to workers and shoppers at Other Avenues. This allowed for a flexible work schedule while I was raising my second child. This work would later become a deli department called "OA's Own."

In the 1980s, when the rents began to increase dramatically and many People's Food System volunteers needed to find paid work, some PFS venues began to hire paid staff. Although there were interesting debates about the issue of paid positions, I personally felt that creating paying jobs in the local economy was consistent with PFS values, so when a paid position became available at OA, I applied and was hired.

My job at OA began at a time when the business was expanding, but was still struggling financially. We did not have steady suppliers for any food items except fresh produce. Our small paid staff were called "daily-task coordinators," a title that every egalitarian could live with. Paid staff, like myself, and experienced volunteers trained a stream of new volunteers to handle tasks that were necessary to keep the doors open. Nonetheless, growth remained slow, and some of us began to see a clear need for even more structure.

I organized our volunteer program by matching people with tasks that suited their interests. Soon the program turned into a close-knit community of folks who lived nearby and walked or biked to the co-op. Some volunteers brought their children, and others came with elderly relatives. The program generated social unity, with food sharing remaining the community-building vehicle it had been in the Food Conspiracy days.

I also worked in the deli department that would become "OA's Own." We made fresh salsa, dips, and sandwiches onsite, and developed fresh food recipes that involved no cooking, as we did not have a permit to cook on the premises. I trained the many volunteers to make these fresh food items—I must have trained dozens of people to prepare our popular OA's Own salsa before I found a steady volunteer, a college professor, who made the salsa for six years.[4]

OA volunteers participated in some of the meetings and events organized by the PFS, including fun-filled potluck dance parties. However, many participants, including myself, kept their distance from the increasingly politically charged discussions within the PFS. While personally intrigued by many of the debates, I had always been less interested in participating in this aspect of the PFS. Instead, I focused on my work at OA and on developing a second cookbook.

Other Avenues group photo, 2016. Back row: David Enos, Luke Larson, Wayne Landers, Nick Patrick, Jane Erbez, Enrique Ramirez, and Steven Watson. Second row: Brennan Murphy, Darryl Dea, Tiffany Acuna, Tulasi Johnson, Layla Gibbon, JB Rumberg, and Kendon Anderson. Third row: Steebalis Ramirez, Alex Miller, Shanta Nimbark Sacharoff, Jeremy Greco, and Chris Julian. Front: Lluis Valls. Photo by Rezz Sacharoff.

For many people, the collapse of the PFS in the 1980s proved traumatic. Many members abruptly left town, and it would be years before I again heard from some of my friends. OA was spared the immediate chaos, partly because our store was at a certain geographical remove from the events, and also because many of OA workers were not involved in PFS politics and did not attend PFS meetings. Nonetheless, OA experienced a shortage of suppliers and sources, which many of our workers and community members found depressing and discouraging. United by a need to focus on our mission of bringing quality food to people and keeping our cooperative spirit alive, the few surviving PFS venues, along with four community food stores and Veritable Vegetable (our wholesale supplier) began to more consciously support one another.

## Culture, Cuisine, and Food Behavior

By this time, I had earned an MA in social psychology from San Francisco State University. My thesis was entitled "The Effects of Vegetarian Cooking Instruction on Food Related Knowledge, Behavior and Attitudes." I used my cooking classes as field work and showed that demonstrating how to prepare nutritious, vegetarian dishes in creative ways and then sharing meals with class members was far more effective in changing people's attitudes toward new foods than lecturing on the superiority of a meatless diet. The experiential ritual of eating together built a sense of community that proved to be a positive platform for assimilating something new.[5]

This research inspired me to write my second cookbook, *The Ethnic Vegetarian Kitchen,* which was published in 1984.[6] This book included vegetarian recipes from many different cultures, as well as a chapter on vegetarian nutrition. After it was published, I taught an interdisciplinary cooking course called "The Culture and Cuisine of India" in the departments of Social Psychology and Home Economics at San Francisco State University.

## Overcoming the 1980s

In the 1980s, as the neighborhood's population changed, Other Avenues began to plan more public events to attract new customers. Cooking classes and educational workshops became popular among shoppers. We also began a door-to-door pamphlet drive, listing fresh and bulk foods that were cheaper at OA than at supermarkets. These promotional activities created an important link between workers and the community during the challenging 1980s.

It was during this period that I reached out to two co-op consultants from Berkeley referred to me by the Cheese Board collective.[7] They helped us create a formal governance structure with written bylaws, an active membership, and a board of directors. We set up a membership signup table in front of the store to rally community support and collected membership fees, which helped ease our cash flow deficit. The governing body was composed of both workers and volunteers from the community. These community members actively participated in meetings and scrutinized OA's financial activities to ensure that we pulled the co-op out of debt.

When the financial situation forced OA to drastically reduce its staff, those of us who remained after the restructuring had to work harder for longer hours. Many of us lived near the store and had small children, so we shared child care near the co-op. To lighten our workload and build solidarity, we planned craft activities, such as "beading bees," and gathered together to quilt baby blankets. My grown children still recall participating in these activities.

In the mid-1990s, to further encourage solidarity among the remaining PFS businesses, an OA volunteer and I joined with a Rainbow Grocery worker to create an umbrella organization called the Inter-collective Organic Union (IOU). Other Avenues and Rainbow collaborated with the Inner Sunset Community Store, the Noe Valley Community Store, Veritable Vegetable, and local organic farmers to host the large San Francisco Organic Harvest Fair in Golden Gate Park in the summers of 1992 and 1993. The festivals educated the public about the benefits of cooperative businesses and organic farming. I still remember fondly the songs of solidarity that bands made up of co-op members played at these events.

For a short time, after my youngest child Sanjay started school, I joined the financially stable Rainbow Grocery Co-op as a worker-member applicant while still working part-time at OA. After working part-time at both co-ops for nearly a year, I left Rainbow and returned to OA, which was closer both to my home and to my heart. The timing of that decision could not have been better, as shortly thereafter our sister co-op Inner Sunset Community Store closed, and many of their customers began to shop at OA. With the business expanding, OA needed experienced workers to train new workers.

Poster advertising Harvest Fair in Golden Gate
Park, 1993. Art by Carlo Denefeld.

In 1999, with OA becoming increasingly financially and organiza-
tionally stable, and with the community's support and blessing, we—
the workers—took the dramatic step of becoming a worker-owned
cooperative.

## Community Connection with Worker-Ownership

To continue and strengthen our connection with other Bay Area co-
ops and shoppers, workers at OA created *Other Ave-News,* a newsletter that is published regularly.[8] We shared co-op-related news, my
seasonal vegetarian recipes, and other information of interest to the
community. My column included not only recipes, but also nutritional information about the ingredients and instructions on how
to store, handle, and prepare foods that might be unfamiliar to our
shoppers, such as okra, Japanese eggplant, and quinoa. I discussed
how to adapt recipes to make them vegan and to lower the fat and
sugar content.

In fall 1999, the popular and expanded *Other Ave-News* announced
the co-op's twenty-fifth anniversary with a history of OA that reflected
the perspectives of three workers. In 2015, the co-op's fortieth anniversary, another three-part series written by three workers recounting
OA's story appeared in *Other Ave-News.*

## A New Era of Local Foods for Local Needs

During the 1990s, the California Sustainable Agriculture (CSA)
groups began to deliver food directly from local farms to various
communities. This was an important service, as more and more small
grocery stores and co-ops were being replaced by chain stores. Some
folks even started to grow fresh food in small inner-city plots and
community gardens. Others started organizing community kitchens and distributing meals. My own contribution to the local food
movement was to initiate and coordinate an OA routine of gathering
and donating withered produce to Food Not Bombs. Carrying on this
family tradition, my daughter Serena currently cooks for Food Not
Bombs in the Mission District of San Francisco, and my son Reyaz
delivers the food culled from the donor stores to the kitchen on his
pedal-powered bike.

Since around 2000, business at Other Avenues and other food
co-ops has been growing. The collapse of the American economy
has created new interest in co-ops. The growing public popularity of

organic food and physical fitness has brought many joggers, walkers, and surfers to the beach, meaning new customers for the Outer Sunset District. A number of new small businesses have opened in the neighborhood, leading to a renaissance of sorts in the community.

I was sad when, in 2007, legal liability issues forced OA to end its volunteer program, displacing an integral part of the co-op family. It was difficult for me to deliver this sad news to those who were near and dear to me, and for volunteers it meant the loss of both a weekly gathering with friends and a way to serve their community. OA proactively created new outreach programs to connect with this loyal community and offered lifetime discounts to many longtime volunteers. With the volunteers gone, OA had to hire more workers and focus seriously on labor issues and on refining the co-op's governance structure. I helped prepare the board to send more workers to conferences and other co-op events to educate ourselves and develop additional tools and techniques.

In 2008, a few workers, including myself, organized the OA community to help the co-op purchase the store's building. Workers and shoppers were able to breathe more freely, knowing that OA had a secure location.

OA's promotional team unites shoppers, suppliers, and neighbors through onsite classes by professionals, including an Ayurveda practitioner and a vegan nutritionist. In addition, Other Avenues sponsors and attends local affairs, such as the Beach Clean-Up, San Francisco Sunday Streets, and the Sunset Community Festival. OA also works with allies, including the San Francisco Mime Troupe and Shaping San Francisco.

In addition, we organize the annual "Chai Party for the Friends of OA" to share news about the co-op's financial status and overall organization. Of course, Other Avenues provides organic refreshments at this event. The growing group of patrons, regular shoppers, ex-volunteers, and interested neighbors remains the backbone of the co-op's community. OA's promotional department, once run by a single individual, is now actively staffed by five to eight workers, and I am confident that OA will continue to share its resources with the community far into the future.

It is gratifying to see that after decades of struggle and the ups and downs of staffing changes, Other Avenues cooperative has a stable group of worker-owners who share business responsibilities and management skills and continue to value a connection with the community. During the years of high turnover and understaffing, new workers shied away from leadership roles and promotional activities, while the old staff struggled with the constant training. Now, with a strong training program in place and a growing leadership, the contributions of all of the co-op worker-members ensure the smooth running of the business.

## Connecting with the Indo-American Community

While working at Other Avenues, I have also connected with the Bay Area's Indo-American community via *India Currents* magazine, which I've written for regularly since 1990, presenting recipes, explaining cooking techniques, providing nutritional information, and discussing the benefits of food sharing.[9]

Over the years, I have seen people's food purchasing patterns, values, and eating habits change, and in response the recipes that I create have evolved. My first recipes used traditional methods and classic ingredients. The 1960s and '70s generation liked many of my from-scratch recipes. As I learned more about other cuisines and cultures in the 1980s, I was inspired to create new recipes that included a fusion of influences from various ethnic cuisines.

Later, the tech generation of the 1990s preferred healthy food, but a meatless menu was less important (and too complicated). Nonetheless, students in my cooking classes made it clear to me that this new generation had an interest in a plant-centered diet. As well, a particular constituency of vegetarians—vegans, who refrain from all animal products—began to grow. In response, I issued a new, revised edition of *Flavors of India* in 1996 that includes vegan alternatives to dishes that traditionally contain milk products.[10]

To meet the needs of a new audience looking for dishes that require less time to prepare yet remain attractive and nutritious, I modified some of my recipes and created new ones. I have addressed special dietary needs with vegan, low-fat, and gluten-free recipes, as well as recipes that focus on seasonal and local foods. Below are three gluten-free vegan examples: one is a vegetable small plate, another is a protein-rich rice entrée, and the third is a fast and easy relish to embellish any entrée.

# ©Small Plate: Ratatouille© (French Vegetable Stew)

Delicately seasoned with fresh herbs, this attractive French dish is hearty and quick to prepare.

- 5–6 tablespoons olive oil
- ¼ cup finely chopped shallots or green onions (white portion only)
- 2 cloves garlic, minced
- 1 red or green bell pepper, deveined, seeded, and cut into thin strips
- ½ large globe eggplant (about ½ pound), unpeeled and cut into bite-sized cubes
- 2 zucchini (about ½ pound), unpeeled and cut into ¼-inch thick slices
- 4 oz. firm tofu cut into cubes (optional)
- 3 tomatoes (½ pound), cut into chunks
- 2 tablespoons tomato paste or thick tomato sauce
- 1 teaspoon each: minced fresh oregano and marjoram or ½ teaspoon each, dried and crumbled
- 1 tablespoon fresh minced basil or 1 teaspoon dried basil, crumbled
- 1 teaspoon fresh rosemary leaves, finely chopped or ½ teaspoon dried and crumbled
- 2 tablespoons red wine or vinegar
- ¼ cup water and more as needed
- 1 tablespoon freshly chopped Italian parsley for garnish

Heat the oil in a large skillet. Add the shallots or green onions and sauté for a few minutes until the onion softens. Add the garlic and cook for 5 minutes. Add the bell pepper, eggplant, and zucchini and fry them for several minutes. Add the optional tofu (which is not traditionally French, but blends in and gives this dish a protein boost). Stir in the tomatoes, tomato paste, herbs, and wine or vinegar. Add the water, cover, and simmer for 10 minutes. Check to see if more water is needed to obtain a stew-like consistency. When done, the vegetables will be soft but keep their shape, and the sauce will be a thick gravy. If it is too dry, add a few tablespoons of water and cook for 5 minutes. Transfer to a serving dish. Top with parsley and serve with bread, pasta, or a rice dish.

Makes eight servings

Recipe adapted from *The Ethnic Vegetarian Kitchen* by Shanta Nimbark Sacharoff.

## ⊚High Protein Peruvian Quinoa⊚ and Basmati Rice Entrée

Both rice and quinoa are easy to digest and quick to prepare. Basmati rice has a unique nutty texture and fragrance that have been attributed to the special soil in which it is grown. Quinoa, an ancient Incan grain, is very high in protein and other nutrients and low in carbohydrates. The stickiness of rice and the nuttiness of the quinoa complement each other.

- 2 cups water
- ½ cup white basmati rice
- ½ cup quinoa
- 1 teaspoon oil (optional)
- ½ teaspoon salt (optional)

Place the rice and quinoa in a strainer and wash and drain them thoroughly. In a saucepan with a tight-fitting lid, bring the water to a boil. Add the optional oil and salt. Add the grains, stir gently, cover, and bring the water to a second boil. Reduce the heat to low and simmer gently for 8 to 10 minutes. Uncover and check to see that the grain is almost cooked. Cover again, and turn off the heat. The steam in the pot will finish cooking the grains in 5 minutes. Serve with vegetables or soup.

Makes four to six servings

*Note: To cook this recipe with brown rice, begin with 2½ cups water. Add the brown rice to the boiling water and set the quinoa aside. Cook the rice covered for 30 minutes over a medium heat and then add the quinoa. Cover and cook both grains together for an additional 10 minutes.*

This is an adapted version of a recipe Shanta Nimbark Sacharoff published in *Indian Currents* in 2014.

# ⊚A Zesty Indian Relish⊚
## Raw Cashew Chutney

Chutney is a zesty relish that commonly accompanies Indian meals. A freshly made chutney can be served to enhance any meal.

- 1 cup raw cashews, soaked in ¾ cups of hot water for 30 minutes
- ½ cup fresh cilantro leaves, stems removed
- 1 tablespoon freshly chopped ginger
- 2 fresh hot jalapeno chilis, seeds and veins removed
- ¼ cup freshly squeezed lemon juice
- ½ teaspoon salt

Place all of the ingredients in a blender or food processor. Blend them for a few minutes to the consistency of crunchy peanut butter, keeping some texture. Let the mixture sit unopened for a few minutes before use. Leftover chutney will keep for a week if refrigerated in a tightly closed container.

Makes 1½ cups

*Variations:*

Peanut Chutney: Use unsalted roasted peanuts in place of cashews. Do not soak the nuts.

This is an adapted version of a recipe Shanta Nimbark Sacharoff published in *Indian Currents*.

## Notes

1. Francis Moore Lappé, *Diet for a Small Planet*, 20th anniversary edition (New York: Ballantine Books, 1991), 61–88.
2. The person who encouraged me to write recipes for publication was Sita Weiner, who was then a member of the Integral Yoga Society in San Francisco.
3. Shanta Nimbark Sacharoff, *Flavors of India* (San Francisco: 101 Productions, 1980).

4. Ray Trautman, a chemistry professor at San Francisco State University, who as a volunteer in OA's Own department, made the fresh salsa for six years.
5. Shanta Nimbark Sacharoff, "The Effects of Vegetarian Cooking Instruction on Food Related Knowledge, Behavior and Attitudes," master's thesis, Social Psychology Department, San Francisco State University, 1988, 29–50.
6. Shanta Nimbark Sacharoff, *The Ethnic Vegetarian Kitchen: Recipes with Guidelines for Nutrition* (San Francisco: 101 Productions, 1984).
7. The two consultants who helped OA in years 1985–87 were Jaques Kaswan and Pete Lee.
8. *Other Ave-News* is published approximately every four months and is regularly updated in the News/Events section of the Other Avenues website, www.otheravenues.coop.
9. *India Currents* is an award-winning monthly magazine published in the San Francisco Bay Area for Indo-Americans and others interested in Southeast Asian culture.
10. Shanta Nimbark Sacharoff, *Flavors of India*, revised edition (Summertown, TN: Book Publishing Company, 1996).

# PART IV
# THE FUTURE IS NOW

Yesterday is but a dream, tomorrow but a vision,
but today well-lived makes every yesterday a dream of
happiness,
and every tomorrow a vision of hope.
Look well, therefore, to this day.
Such is the salutation to the dawn.
—*A Sanskrit proverb*

THE AMERICAN PEOPLE are ready to create new jobs where the fruits of their labor are shared by the workers, instead of being snatched away disproportionately by the powerful corporate 1%. In *Forbes*, Cameron Keng pointed out that if Apple was a worker cooperative, each employee—even the lowest paid staff member—would have earned at least $403,000 in 2012. He further asserted that if a large number of businesses, each with thousands of employees, could operate as worker co-ops in Mondragon, Spain, enterprises of any scale anywhere could function as worker cooperatives.

> *"Worker cooperatives answer the question*
> *we've all asked ourselves—what's the*
> *point of working hard for someone else?"[1]*
> —Cameron Keng

## Co-ops Rise Again
Since the earliest days of the industrial revolution, capitalist forces have increasingly exploited labor. This situation continues today, as

evidenced by the rising income gap between workers, managers, employers, and owners. Twentieth-century author George Orwell suggested limiting the income gap between the lowest paid workers and the highest paid workers to no more than ten times. Compare that with today's corporate numbers; the compensation received by S&P 500 CEOs in 2012 was on average 354 times the income of their lowest paid workers![2]

Just as was the case in the 1960s and '70s, the average American worker today is economically disempowered. But one thing has definitely changed; regularly using social media to exchange views about their working conditions allows today's workers to form connections in an unprecedented way. As the sociologist Marshall McLuhan predicted in the 1960s, the "global village" has brought people together with a heightened sense of urgency and a growing desire to find new solutions. The new media technologies could prove to be a strong catalyst for social change.[3]

Throughout American history, people have started cooperatives to give themselves power and a voice in their work. By accessing public works funding under the New Deal, co-ops helped improve the gloomy economy of the 1930s. The co-ops of the 1960s and '70s shaped local economies with a "storefront revolution." The co-op movement of the 1980s and '90s built the network necessary for surviving the takeover of "real food" by health food market chains. Today we are seeing the rise of cooperatives that establish jobs built on workplace democracy, while addressing global environmental issues.

> *"It's a coalition of . . . people working for the community. . . . [They] are mad as hell but do something about it . . . [They] get organized and find . . . a way around it. . . . you know, my mama told me that two wrongs don't make a right, but three left turns do."[4]*
> —Jim Hightower

Over the years, co-ops have risen and fallen, influenced by socioeconomic and cultural forces, but the movement has never disappeared. Co-ops have always been embraced by progressive people who

believe in fair labor practices and alternative solutions to the problems wrought by capitalism. However, the current co-op movement is
different from the previous waves. Current co-ops are more pragmatic
than their 1970s counterparts. They connect with the marketplace to
create jobs, while maintaining their democratic identity. Newer co-ops
ally closely with other small businesses, including fair-trade vendors
and local farmers and entrepreneurs. These new cooperators seem increasingly inclined to build and decentralize leadership in ways that
some of their predecessors didn't. The new wave of co-ops in the San
Francisco Bay Area, which has been growing since the late 1990s, by
and large takes the form of worker cooperatives.[5]

The co-op movement in the San Francisco Bay Area has always
been strong, but it has not been immune to the boom and bust cycles.
After blossoming in the 1970s, co-ops had difficulty surviving in the
harsh economic environment of the 1980s. However, the co-ops that
did survive imbued a variety of small businesses with a fresh enthusiasm for reviving the movement, allowing the current strong wave of
worker-owned cooperatives to germinate.[6] In 2015, fifty-eight worker-owned co-ops were listed on the Bay Area Worker Cooperatives
map, including retail food co-ops, food service businesses, publishers,
a printer, bike repair and sales shops, tech services, house cleaning
services, and schools.[7] A number of the old, established consumer co-
ops in the Bay Area are also doing well.[8]

In addition, a large network of organizations has been created in
the Bay Area to support the new movement. This network also acts to
connect co-op organizations in various regions of the United States.
Together, these organizations are developing a nationwide co-op
movement that is diverse in both membership and scale. This network's vision is to create many more democratic and sustainable cooperatives in the United States and around the world.

In addition to creating jobs, building co-ops is a form of political
activism, and perhaps this is nowhere as true as it is in the food sector.
No group has been more undermined by the growth of giant food
corporations in the United States than food service workers, including
restaurant workers, retail food store workers, farmworkers, and food
assembly line workers. Progressive media have documented the harsh
and unsafe working conditions and extremely low wages of most young
retail food clerks and food service workers in the United States. They
note that while the retail food industry has flourished in California,

the state's food retail workers' wages have declined, and their working conditions have deteriorated. Adjusted for inflation, food sector workers, who have little or no bargaining power, are earning less than what they earned two decades ago.[9] Co-op organizations are aware of these conditions and are eager to help provide a more sustainable and safer work environment for those employed in the retail food industry.

## Notes

1. Cameron Keng, "If Apple Was a Worker Cooperative," *Forbes*, December 18, 2014, http://www.forbes.com/sites/cameronkeng/2014/12/18/if-apple-was-a-worker-cooperative-each-employee-would-earn-at-least-403k/#2c04c0ac56cc.
2. Deborah Hargreaves, "Can We Close the Gap?" *New York Times*, March 29, 2014, http://opinionator.blogs.nytimes.com/2014/03/29/can-we-close-the-pay-gap/?_r=0.
3. Marshall McLuhan, *The Gutenberg Galaxy: The Making of Typographic Man* (Toronto, Canada: University of Toronto Press, 1962); Marshal McLuhan, *Understanding Media: The Extensions of Man* (New York: McGraw-Hill, 1964).
4. Jim Hightower in conversation with Bill Moyers on *Watch and Listen*, April 30, 2010, www.pbs.org/moyers/journal/04302010/watch2.html.
5. "Democracy at Work Press Kit," http://institute.coop/news/democracy-work-instituteusfwc-press-kit.
6. Ibid.
7. An updated (2015) Network of Bay Area Worker Cooperatives (NoBAWC) list can be found in the Appendices.
8. A partial list of old established co-ops of the San Francisco Bay Area, including consumer-owned food co-ops, can be found in the Appendices.
9. Neil Irwin, "Why American Workers without Much Education Are Being Hammered," *New York Times*, "The Upshot," April 21, 2015, http://www.nytimes.com/2015/04/22/upshot/why-workers-without-much-education-are-being-hammered.html; Saru, Jayaraman and the Food Labor Research Center, "Shelved: How Wages and Working Conditions for California Food Retail Workers Have Declined as the Industry Has Thrived," 2014, http://laborcenter.berkeley.edu/pdf/2014/Food-Retail-Report.pdf; and Saru Jayaraman, "The Rise of the Low-Wage Restaurant Industrial Complex," *MSNBC*, September 13, 2014, http://www.msnbc.com/msnbc/the-rise-the-low-wage-restaurant-industry-hurts-the-economy.

# CHAPTER 7
## SUSTAINING FOOD CO-OPS

HISTORICALLY, THE CO-OP movement has supported both a clean food environment and fair labor practices. Food co-ops have always had strong relationships with farmers and have shared their concerns about the future of small farms. The mutual bond among farmers, consumers, and food workers is even stronger today. On a street level, co-op workers, shoppers, and food suppliers joined to lobby for GM labeling. Co-ops promote local farmers on their websites, posting information about their sustainable practices. Product displays often include signs such as: "Organic flowers from Full Belly Farms." For their part, local organic farmers connect consumers with co-ops by providing information about the stores that carry their products. Co-ops, with their commitment to fair labor practices, also serve to introduce many consumers to products available through fair-trade farmers and vendors. The end result is a new coalition of food activists that includes consumers, food sector workers, restaurant chefs, and farmers, all working toward a healthy and more sustainable and local food system.

Despite the renewed link with workers in related fields and growing public support for the co-op movement in the Bay Area, food co-ops face challenges that were not major issues in the past. For example, the increased demand for organic food has given rise to large chains of "natural food" supermarkets that carry food in larger volumes than is possible for small co-ops. The extremely high rents in the Bay Area also make it difficult for food co-ops to operate with a low enough margin to be competitive. As a result, only a handful of the once numerous 1970s food co-op stores remain open in the San Francisco Bay Area.[1]

This is not, however, true for the entire state of California, where the Center for California Cooperative Development reports that food co-ops are experiencing a rare boom. In the past ten years, approximately ten new food co-ops have started in California, and a few more are in the planning stage.[2]

Co-opportunity Natural Foods, Santa Monica, 1976.
Photo by Philip Clayton-Thompson.

While new retail food co-ops have not been feasible in the Bay Area in recent years, a handful of new co-ops have emerged in food service sectors over the past two decades, some with the support and inspiration of the old food co-ops. For example, University of California students in Berkeley opened a retail food co-op in 2010, and more student co-ops are under development across the state. Meanwhile, drawing upon the Spanish Mondragon co-op model, a series of Arizmendi bakeries has been established in the Bay Area. A fair number of worker-owned cooperatives have also opened in non-food sectors.[3] While these visionary new cooperatives compete with private businesses, their goals are different; they are focused on supporting social change in their communities, and not simply on their own survival.

## Lessons from the Past

Both new and existing co-ops continue to learn from the past. New co-ops carefully study the weaknesses—inadequate capitalization, lack of member participation, poor business management, internal conflict—that contributed to past failures. Instead of forming large centralized governing bodies, as the late People's Food System tried to do, current co-ops prefer to remain decentralized.[4] In fact, this new "localism" is their strength. For example, the burgeoning Arizmendi Association is made up of small independently run bakeries. Although decentralized, like their ancestors, the current Bay Area co-ops share historical information and discuss new developments, using both social media and organized events.

New co-ops have also learned that they need to distinguish themselves from other businesses by emphasizing the centrality of workplace democracy in their models. The survivors have taught the new co-ops that they need to understand industry trends. The new food co-ops have learned to prioritize running a business, including adequately training new workers and providing quality customer service, rather than having food politics dominate the workplace. While engaging with their communities to support an overall progressive agenda, co-op workers understand that exemplary customer service and attention to their communities' immediate needs are essential to co-op success.

## The Cooperative Support Network in the San Francisco Bay Area

A strong network of organizations has arisen in the San Francisco Bay Area to serve the rapidly growing interest in co-op business models. These organizations share resources and professional tools with one another to help create new co-ops, support existing co-ops, and build a national movement. They link co-ops with other nonprofit and community resources, including legal and financial institutions, in much the same way the People's Food System did in the 1970s; in fact, some of the founders of these organizations acknowledge their debt to the inspiration and guidance provided by the PFS.[5]

Many of the Bay Area organizations that support co-op development are described below, but it's a list that keeps growing, as new individuals join the movement and new agencies arise. Some of these organizations focus on the Bay Area, some on California as a whole, and a certain number provide services nationwide and beyond. These organizations conduct crucial research and provide essential information about the resources available from other co-ops and allied agencies. Using referral systems and joint events, they share the results of their work, effectively becoming a clearinghouse of information for every type and size of cooperative. This network also educates the public about the benefits of co-ops and lobbies for pro-co-op legislation at both state and federal levels.

*The Network of Bay Area Worker Cooperatives or NoBAWC* (pronounced "No Boss") is a grassroots organization that was created in 1996 by a group of democratic workplaces, the majority of them worker-owned co-ops in the San Francisco Bay Area. On its 2015 map, NoBAWC lists fifty-eight workplaces that are co-ops, transitional co-ops (those on their way to becoming co-ops), or organizations that, although not worker co-ops, integrate co-op principles in their governance. NoBAWC operates on a shoestring budget, supported by membership fees, but not all workplaces on the NoBAWC list are dues-paying members. Two part-time staff members and a volunteer board of directors do most of the organizational work.

NoBAWC's mission is to connect its members to one another, so that they can share organizational information, improve mutual solidarity, and promote sustainability. Meetings where members of all worker-owned co-ops can exchange ideas are an essential part of this connection. The meetings often feature a guest speaker who leads a discussion on a relevant topic.

NoBAWC's website provides basic information necessary for starting a co-op or for converting an existing business into a co-op. The website also offers an excellent library of resources about co-ops and co-op-related services, as well as providing updated links to regional, national, and international co-op organizations. The NoBAWC newsletter, *Collective Action*, covers both local co-ops and co-ops from around the world. For example, did you know that Cuban cooperatives play a major role in the island's economic development? Check out "Cuba Going Coop" in the March 2015 issue of *Collective Action*.[6]

NoBAWC worked with the Community Congress of San Francisco in 2010, campaigning for the city government to support co-op development. NoBAWC also assisted in the establishment of co-op businesses in the city of Richmond. In 2015, NoBAWC supported the "Resolution Supporting the Development of Worker Cooperatives in Oakland." Nationally, NoBAWC has taken a stance on environmental issues, including limiting and labeling genetically modified foods (GMOs). A NoBAWC staff member represented the San Francisco Bay Area worker cooperatives at the United Nation's 2012 celebration of the International Year of Cooperatives.

Davis Food Coop, 1970s. Photo by Ann M. Evans.

*The California Center for Cooperative Development (CCCD)* started as an educational program at the University of California, Davis, to study the role of co-ops in California's economy. It closed in 2004 and reopened as a nonprofit organization in 2007, its mission being to address California's socioeconomic needs by developing cooperatives. Some of the CCCD's current staff and board members came from the former University of California program, and the CCCD continues to receive the assistance of UC Davis university interns.

The CCCD serves all types of co-ops, including consumer co-ops, worker-owned co-ops, student-run co-ops, housing co-ops, producer co-ops, and food-buying clubs. The CCCD organizes an annual "Co-op Day at the Capitol" in Sacramento, offering Bay Area co-ops the opportunity to educate legislators about cooperatives' contributions to the local economy.

The CCCD's annual California Co-op Conference invites professionals from around the nation to share co-op development tools. The 2015 CCCD conference in Sacramento, was attended by approximately 130 cooperators and co-op developers. The CCCD also organizes an annual conference for the directors of agricultural cooperatives, and is a sponsor of the annual Western Worker Co-op Conference organized by the United States Federation of Worker Cooperatives (USFWC). The CCCD and the USFWC are both members of Cooperation Works!, a national network of Cooperative Development Centers.

The CCCD reports a growing interest in food co-ops on college campuses and in rural communities, both of which are "food deserts." Community Supported Agriculture (CSA) deliveries and local farmers markets bring seasonal food to these areas, but this is not sufficient. The people are increasingly aware of their need for, and their right to, healthy food; during the 2014 CCCD Conference, a food-buying club requested support to start a food co-op in rural Lake County, California.

In 2015, the CCCD organized a gathering of immigrant and refugee farmers and gardeners to take part in New Roots training programs for beginner and disadvantaged farmers, including California's ALBA (Agriculture and Land-Based Training Association, described on page 143) program.[7]

Part of the CCCD staff's workday is spent responding to queries from the public about various cooperative models. The director of CCCD, Kim Coontz, argues that the current surge of interest in co-ops is a sign of people's distrust of the government during times of national crisis. Disappointed by "business as usual," the public has increasingly turned to local alternatives. She adds that to meet the rising demand for information, the three Bay Area-based co-op organizations (NoBAWC, CCCD, and USFWC) increasingly pool their resources, but she stresses that more collaboration is still needed.[8]

Fort Bragg, California, 1972. Photo by David J. Thompson.

*The United States Federation of Worker Cooperatives (USFWC)* is an Oakland-based organization made up of worker cooperatives, democratic workplaces, network organizations, and individuals that work to support the development of worker cooperatives. Founded by the Regional Worker Cooperatives of the United States in 2004, its mission is to help sustain a burgeoning co-op movement by providing education, advocacy, and development. Since the economic downturn of 2008, the staff has seen a growing interest in cooperatives across the country. To provide educational workshops, the federation sponsors several large regional and national conferences annually, as well as smaller local events.

The USFWC continues to grow, and its annual national conference continues to draw more worker cooperatives and their supporters every year. In 2014, the USFWC reported a membership of more than one hundred workplaces, representing more than 1,600 American workers, and that year its national conference in Chicago was attended by more than 400 people, including co-op members, co-op developers, funding groups, and allied businesses. To encourage local co-op development, the event rotates to different parts of the country. In 2008, for example, the USFWC chose New Orleans for the conference, to support its residents' efforts to rebuild the city in the wake of the disastrous Hurricane Katrina of 2007. Some co-op workers remained in New Orleans for a week after the conference to help and to see how cooperative models might contribute to the city's recovery.[9]

Who inquires about co-ops and why? An USFWC staff member tells us that groups wanting to start co-ops call the USFWC with "how to" questions during the early planning stages, hoping to avoid common mistakes. Owners who hope to avoid having to sell their small business to a faceless corporation inquire about converting into a co-op or a worker-owned business. Individuals and nonprofit organizations that want to help co-ops, or need help from co-ops, call USFWC with legal and financial questions. As unlikely as it would seem, the USFWC even gets queries from state and federal agencies that are looking for alternatives to failing traditional models.[10]

The USFWC has set some goals for sustainable co-op growth: (1) to increase co-op membership, (2) to replicate successful co-op models in areas other than retail business, and (3) to grow relationships with financial institutions and to establish links among co-ops to create financial security.

The USFWC amplifies its members' voices when addressing local and national legislation. For example, the USFWC recently worked with other co-op organizations to draft legislation that would change the current co-op statute to establish a permanent and visible legal status for worker cooperatives. AB816 passed in 2015, providing a clear legal template for worker co-ops. The regularly updated online resource directory includes a library of co-op literature and research and a USFWC membership list that helps users find co-ops or co-op development services in their area. The USFWC sponsors webinars on issues like policies and procedures for handling worker accountability in co-op settings.

The growth of the USFWC stimulated a new project, the Democracy at Work Institute (DAWI), which serves economically marginalized communities. To address increasing demand, in 2013, the DAWI became a separate nonprofit organization dedicated to co-op development in under-served communities.

The USFWC and the DAWI remain affiliated and share office space, but they play distinctly different roles. The USFWC is primarily a membership-funded organization that provides services to its member co-ops. The DAWI is grant-funded and provides services to the public, to new co-ops, and to co-op developers to stimulate co-op growth, particularly in disadvantaged communities. The DAWI has secured ongoing financial support for its work in building sustainable local economies in low-income areas.

Arizmendi Bakery San Francisco, 2015. Photo by Rezz Sacharoff.

*The Arizmendi Association of Cooperatives (AAC)* is a Bay Area-based umbrella organization made up of a number of retail food service co-operatives.[11] It is named after José María Arizmendiarrieta, a priest who inspired the creation of the successful Mondragon cooperatives in the Basque Country in Spain. Each Arizmendi co-op operates autonomously, but accounting, legal services, training, and education are centralized. The member co-ops are connected by a common vision of running a successful business, while supporting the development of new co-ops in the Bay Area.

In 1971, the first Arizmendi collective, the Cheese Board in North Berkeley, was converted by its two owners from a private retail cheese business into a worker-owned collective, with the six employees coming on board as equal partners. In 1985, the Cheese Board opened a nearby, independently operated pizzeria, with the two co-ops sharing some resources. Both remain successful businesses today.

In 1995, a group from the Cheese Board organized the Arizmendi Association in the hope of increasing the number of democratic workplaces in the Bay Area. They developed a unique franchise model, fashioned after the Mondragon co-ops in Spain and modified to fit the Arizmendi Association's needs. Unlike corporate franchise paradigms, where expansion is based on the sale of a business model for a substantial sum of money, plus royalties on sales, the co-op bakeries share recipes and business models to encourage increased workplace democracy. In addition to the original Cheese Board Collective and the Cheese Board Pizzeria co-op, there are now five other Arizmendi bakeries in various locations in the San Francisco Bay Area. Each member co-op contributes a portion of its surplus to the AAC to support existing co-ops and to promote new one. Established co-ops contribute a larger percentage of their surplus than newer, less financially stable ones. The AAC is governed by two representatives from each member business and a board of directors; these groups jointly decide how to allocate the resources.

Most Arizmendi bakeries have a multigenerational staff, and the diverse issues that this brings to the forefront serves to strengthen the collectives. Some Cheese Board workers have been part of the collective for over three decades, while newly hired workers tend to be young. When asked about the future of Arizmendi, one long-time Cheese Board worker expressed a concern about the increasingly expensive real estate market, which is making it difficult for the younger

Makes Loaves Not War, at Arizmendi Bakery, San Francisco. Worker-owners Ryan Lathouwers and Sue Lopez. Photo by Rezz Sacharoff.

workers to live in Berkeley, despite decent wages. As a result, these workers might fail to develop the same sense of community with the neighborhood they serve as the previous generation.[12] For her part, a young worker expressed concern about how the Cheese Board's structure would evolve once the older generation passes the torch.[13]

The AAC participates in co-op events and works with other organizations to advance co-op education and to support pro-co-op legislative reform. Their leadership sees great potential in the current growth of co-ops and hopes to create an advisory board composed of co-op workers and organizations. In the future, the AAC envisions venturing beyond food co-ops to embrace other cooperative enterprises.[14]

> "We have never thought of ourselves as in the business of building bakery cooperatives, but building an engine for accelerating cooperative growth.[15] . . . For me, worker cooperatives are not simply businesses; they are democracy demonstration projects, schools for democracy, laboratories for democracy and organizing bases for democracy"[16]
> —Tim Huet of Arizmendi Association

The AAC's website includes a comprehensive Worker Cooperative Resource List, and the AAC actively supports the Bay Area's new co-op program called the Worker Co-op Academy (started in 2014 as a joint project of the Sustainable Economies Law Center, Project Equity, the Green Collar Communities Clinic, and Laney College) with a mission to create quality jobs in a co-op setting for low- and moderate-income workers. The Worker Co-op Academy offers a ten-week course in co-op creation, conversion, and development, with a curriculum focused on legal, management, and cultural issues.[17]

*Cooperative Food Empowerment Development (CoFed)* was launched in the Bay Area in 2010 by college students who had become increasingly aware of sociopolitical issues surrounding the accessibility of healthy food in their communities. Its mission is to set up student-run food co-ops across the nation. Given that students face high unemployment and heavy debt after graduation, food co-ops on campuses would be an ideal solution for creating at least a few decent jobs and providing healthy food. During the 1970s, there were a number of food co-ops on Bay Area campuses; today, there are only two: one near the University of California, Berkeley, and the other at the University of California, Santa Cruz.

To empower students and build solidarity, CoFed staff members network with allied agencies and youth organizations, such as the North American Students of Cooperation (NASCO) and the USA Cooperative Youth Council (USACYC), to organize skill-sharing events that connect students with mentors and peers. In 2015, CoFed's Summer Learning Institute in Oakland trained twenty-one students from across the country in co-op governance, business planning, and community involvement.[18] CoFed maintains a database, The Commons, which includes updates about the technical tools necessary for starting food co-ops.

A CoFed staff member said that food activists on college campuses are aware that some of the communities adjoining campuses also lack access to healthy food. They see their mission as including food and justice in the surrounding area and hope to work with their neighbors to create cooperative ventures.[19] She added that establishing food co-ops on community colleges with diverse populations would increase both the prospect of decent jobs and access to healthy food for college students.

> "The food co-op's movement is tied to 'the movement.' It's not the natural foods movement, it's not the Occupy Movement, it's not a food-co-op movement; it is all of those and more. . . . It is a movement to bend the arc closer to justice. Economic Justice. Food Justice. Racial Justice. Social Justice. Community Wealth . . . connected elements to liberating our potential and creating community-owned food systems."[20]
> —Farzana Serang of CoFed

Students are a transient population, and as a result it is a challenge to convince them of the long-term benefits of food co-ops on local economies. However, CoFed's staff is optimistic that their efforts will lead to the establishment of a number of student-run food co-ops in California and across the nation over the next few years. The Bay Area's network of co-op support organizations sees the importance of the coming generation of cooperators being the vanguard of the movement and provides CoFed members a platform for sharing their concerns and their visions for the future development of the co-op movement. Food co-ops, including Other Avenues, donate food to CoFed's summer program, as well as offering co-op tours.

## Food and Justice Organizations in the San Francisco Bay Area

The socio-economic issues surrounding the sustainable growth of healthy food and its distribution to all of the people are key questions for the Bay Area's population. Like other civil rights issues, food activism asserts that good food is a human right and not a privilege. Food co-ops, being agents of social change, recognize the connections between sustainable agriculture, fair food distribution, and human health.

The San Francisco Bay Area, the home of collectivism, has historically supported the food and justice movement. The Food Conspiracy opened storefronts and created the People's Food System to make healthy food available to more people. As discussed in Chapter 2, the PFS's greatest challenge was to include more than just "white middle-class youth." Some folks encouraged co-ops to hire marginalized workers, and others opened co-ops in underserved communities. Nonetheless, decades later, food insecurity remains as prevalent as ever; many people are hungry. The work of food and justice activism remains unfinished.

Similarly, the plight of small farmers and farmworkers is an important human rights issue that requires more attention. Historically, food co-ops have allied with small farmers in their struggle to reclaim land from agribusiness and to acquire safe working conditions. Food co-ops began to buy food directly from farmers, and co-op workers rallied against the unsafe farm practices that affected migrant workers. These joint efforts of farmworkers, farmers, co-op workers, and consumers achieved some positive change, but more collaboration between concerned citizens and co-ops is required to fight the escalating powers of agribusiness, as it continues to drench farmlands with harmful chemicals and fill supermarkets with genetically modified foods.

Food co-op workers and consumers are currently focusing attention on food security, food safety, and farming issues. France Moore Lappé long ago asserted that while we do have enough food to feed the world's population, we do not grow and distribute that food in a sustainable manner, and that remains true. Similarly, we have the farmers necessary to till the land, but many of them have been reduced to disenfranchised farmworkers. A declining number of small farmers struggles with inadequate means and an uncertain future.

So, what are cooperatives currently doing to address food and justice issues in the Bay Area? An increasing number of co-ops buy food from small local farmers, and some of them donate produce to nonprofit organizations, including soup kitchens and food banks. Others set up discount programs that allow people to buy food at a reduced price. Some of them support community gardens where people can grow their own food, and others offer workshops on issues like nutrition and cooking on limited food budget. Some citizens lobby to bring fresh food to communities that are food deserts, and some workers are active around agricultural issues, such as restricting and/or properly labeling genetically modified foods. These actions constitute an interconnected food and justice initiative.

What follows is a list of just a few of the many tireless Bay Area organizations working to keep food security issues on the table. New groups continue to be formed, sometimes spontaneously, to bring healthy food to all communities.

*Food First,* or *the Institute for Food and Development Policy,* was founded in the 1970s by food and justice advocates Frances Moore Lappé and Joseph Collins to dispel the myth that world hunger is caused by actual food scarcity and to point out that the real reason for the food insecurity among world populations is unequal food distribution and irresponsible agricultural practices. The institute eventually expanded its base so that it could conduct research and raise funds to help address these problems.

In 2008, Food First supported the creation of the Oakland Food Policy Council (OFPC), a coalition of concerned citizens, allied organizations, farmers, restaurateurs, and policy makers united to address local food security issues. The council brings together community members and elected officials in an effort to persuade city government to support venues like the Mandela Marketplace and to help bring healthy food to all of Oakland's residents. To make healthy food more accessible, the OFPC supports and promotes farmers markets, healthy corner stores, food co-ops, urban gardens, and local food sources.[21]

> *"Basically, [food security is] the idea that people should have the resources and the access to provide food for themselves. . . . If you tell people to eat a healthy diet but they don't have a grocery store . . . and don't have a car, there is no way to access it."*[22]
> —Andy Fisher, executive director of the Community Food Security Coalition

*Mandela Marketplace* in West Oakland is the outcome of a community-based initiative to address food and justice issues in the neighborhood.[23] West Oakland is a diverse community with a lot of potential, but it suffers from a high unemployment rate and food scarcity. Many grocery stores have moved to more affluent neighborhoods, leaving this area with corner stores that primarily stock liquor. In 2009, Mandela Marketplace, a nonprofit organization, opened with the goal of accessing healthy food and creating safe and secure employment, in a partnership with local residents, farmers, and community-based businesses. In order to build a sustainable local food system, the Mandela Marketplace founders developed several synergistic food enterprises, including deliveries from local farmers, farm stands, and a retail food co-op called the Mandela Foods Cooperative.

Mandela Marketplace links small family farmers to food stands, local enterprises, and corner grocery stores. Collectively, they purchase approximately 40 percent of the fresh produce grown on these local farms. A number of other West Oakland neighborhood initiatives modeled on the Mandela Marketplace are currently on the drawing board. The Mandela Marketplace has received numerous awards and government grants recognizing its important contribution to this crucial community work.[24]

Mandela Foods Cooperative with worker-owner James Bell, 2015.
Photo by Rezz Sacharoff.

*Mandela Foods Cooperative (MFC)* is owned by workers who live in the neighborhood. MFC secures healthy food for the residents and supports the local economy by creating jobs. This area, previously only served by fast-food chains and corner stores, now has several businesses selling fresh organic food.

> *"A small group of women demanded access to fresh produce and healthy food in the neighborhood. After several years of community organizing, nine founding members opened Mandela Foods Cooperative in 2009 with the support of many community members and Mandela Market Place."*[25]
> —The "Short Story" segment of the Mandela Foods Cooperative's website

In spite of being a fairly young business, the Mandela Foods Cooperative is well stocked with fresh produce and many organic food items. It also has a good section of packaged grocery items and healthy frozen meals. Zella's Soulful Kitchen, a separate business located inside the co-op, is a good fit, catering and selling healthy ready-to-eat soul food to the residents.

In spite of its limited inventory of grocery items—a typical problem for a young food store—a worker-owner said that the community supports the MFC because of what the co-op stands for. The small market stocks food products from more than twenty-five local vendors and farmers. The worker-owner I spoke with said that finding the right workers to staff the co-op has also been challenging, because in our modern culture so many people want a job where they clock in and clock out. It has sometimes proven difficult to get the message across to applicants that being a worker-owner is more than just doing a job and getting a paycheck. That said, he was quick to stress that the goal remains for new MFC employees to become worker-owners after an initial training and evaluation process.[26]

*Food Not Bombs (FNB)* is distinctly different from other free-food programs. Now a global organization, FNB was started in Massachusetts by anti-nuclear protesters in 1980.[27] They began to regularly congregate in outdoor settings to share meals and to discuss nonviolent means of social change. Recognizing that hunger is not caused by food shortage but by unfair food distribution, FNB members began cooking vegetarian meals from culls (imperfect produce that would otherwise be thrown away) donated by co-ops and restaurants and offering them to the public for free. Inspired by the 1970s food co-op consensus model of decision-making, FNB is made up of leaderless collectives.

*The San Francisco Vegetarian Society (SFVS)*, a local chapter of the World Vegetarian Society, advocates a plant-based diet to address world hunger and to protect animal rights.[28] Vegetarian Society members support food co-ops, as green businesses offering a large variety of plant-based products, and the SFVS regularly publishes co-op news and publicizes co-op events on its busy website. SFVS members also network with local communities, attending public events like the annual SF Pride parade to distribute literature and vegetarian food. Thousands of people attend SFVS's annual World Vegetarian Weekend, featuring vegan food booths, cooking demonstrations, and vegetarian educators like John Robbins and Howard Lyman. Other

Avenues, which offers SFVS members a discount on their purchases, is a regular participant at the event.

Golden Hill Food Co-op, San Diego, 1978.
Photo by David J. Thompson.

The creation of a *Food Justice Certification Program* that determines labor standards for farmworkers and lists farms that follow fair labor practices is an issue being addressed by some small organic farmers. In addition to food insecurity, working conditions for farmers and farmworkers in California, a state that grows much of the country's food, raise serious labor justice concerns. Migrant laborers' poor working conditions are aggravated by their fear of deportation and their lack of legal protection.[29] As part of this certification program, the farmers will also call upon retail food shoppers to support livable wages and safe working conditions for farmworkers. For these farmers, who face their own work challenges and financial insecurity, the issue is as important as organic food certification. They will doubtless get the backing of additional farmers, co-op workers, and consumers who already support legislation to help migrant workers obtain citizenship.

*The Agriculture and Land-Based Training Association (ALBA)*, in Monterey County, California, trains and leases land to immigrant and seasonal farmworkers who aspire to become organic farmers. The ALBA started in 2000 as part of a government anti-poverty program, and later became a farm cooperative, before evolving into a training program. Currently, the ALBA creates jobs for organic farmworkers and secures them healthy organic food.[30]

All over California, and particularly in the Bay Area, the food and justice movement is growing, and the impact of its efforts to secure food for people and fair labor practices for farm and food sector workers are being felt across the nation. Co-op workers continue to place sustainable food initiatives on state ballots as part of the struggle to keep the Bay Area's food system one that is "For People, Not for Profit." From time to time, even the USDA supports the movement on one issue or another—not on the same scale that it defends agribusiness, mind you.

Meanwhile, throughout the Bay Area, informal groups, including urban gardeners and farmers markets, educate the public about organic food. A community garden program in the Mission District of San Francisco offers its surplus produce to the public on a free food pickup day every summer. There are also many charitable organizations distributing food and prepared meals to the needy via soup kitchens and food banks.[31]

The agro-giants continue to hold on to their power, but everywhere citizens are collaborating to demand food and justice. The roots of our alternative food system run deep. The seminal work of the Diggers and the Food Conspiracy's legacy will keep flowering for generations to come, as the current strength of cooperatives shows. However, more collaborative work is needed before cooperatives are secure and sustainable and food and justice issues are adequately addressed—both here in the Bay Area and beyond.

> *"Cooperatives are a reminder to the international community that it is possible to pursue both economic viability and social responsibility."*[32]
> —Ban Ki-moon, UN secretary-general

144     Other Avenues Are Possible

Sacramento Natural Foods, 1983. Photo by David J. Thompson.

## Notes

1. View the food co-op list on pp. 165–66 to witness the lack of growth in retail food co-op stores in the San Francisco Bay Area.
2. Luis Sierra, "California food Co-ops in Rare Boom," *The Vine*, February/March 2014. Luis Sierra is the assistant executive director of the California Center for Cooperative Development. *The Vine* is the BriarPatch Co-op's community newsletter.
3. See the new 2015 list of the Bay Area's worker-owned cooperatives in the NoBAWC list in the Appendices.
4. Refer to Chapter 2 for the analysis of the PFS's struggle to centralize, pp. 37–51.
5. Author conversation with Melissa Hoover, 2011. Melissa is currently the director of Democracy at Work Institute. When we talked, she was the director of United States Federation of Worker Cooperatives.
6. "Cuba Going Coop," *Collective Action* 2, no. 2, March 2015, http://nobawc.org/wp-content/uploads/2015/04/Collective_Action_March_20151.pdf.
7. Gwenael Engelskirchen, "CCCD Convenes Education Summit for Refugee and Immigrant Farmer Training Program," *Co-op Connections*, 2016, 1–2.
8. Author interview with California Center Cooperative Development's director Kim Coontz at the California Center for Cooperative Development Conference, May 2015.

9. The author, who was among those who remained in New Orleans for the week, witnessed the collective enthusiasm of the participating cooperators, who attended community gardening and co-op planning meetings with New Orleans residents.

10. Author interview with Amy Johnson, co-director of US Federation of Worker Cooperatives, May 2015.

11. A list of Arizmendi bakeries and Arizmendi Association of Cooperatives contact information can be found in the Appendices. Also, see www.arizmendi.coop.

12. Author interview with Steve Sutcher of the Cheese Board Collective, December 2015. Steve has worked at the Cheese Board for more than three decades.

13. Author interview with Omri Avraham of Cheese Board in December 2015.

14. Author interview with Tim Huet, May 2015. Tim is an Arizmendi Association of Cooperatives board member.

15. Tim Huet, "From Mondragon Networking to Franchising: The Arizmendi Association Model of Financing," *Grassroots Economic Organizing (GEO) Newsletter* 2, no. 12, 2013: http://www.geo.coop/story/mondragon-networking-franchising.

16. Tim Huet, "A Cooperative Manifesto," *GEO Newsletter* 61, http://www.geo.coop/archives/huetman604.htm.

17. For more information on the Worker Coop Academy, visit http://www.theselc.org/worker-coop-academy.

18. Much of the information regarding CoFed comes from an author interview with its director Farzana Serang, July 2015, and from its website, www.cofed.coop.

19. In a September 2015 e-mail communication with the author, Farzana Serang, director of CoFed, stated that students from minority backgrounds are disproportionately represented among students with larger debts and less access to healthy food.

20. Statement by Farzana Serang of CoFed in an e-mail communication with the author.

21. For more information on Oakland Food Policy Council, visit http://www.oaklandfood.org.

22. Andy Fisher, executive director of the Community Food Security Coalition quoted in Tara Duggan, "Bay Area/Bringing Healthy Produce to Poor Neighborhoods/Food Activists, Small Farmers lead Project," *SF Gate*, July 16, 2014, http://www.sfgate.com/bayarea/article/BAY-AREA-Bringing-healthy-produce-to-poor-2741215.php.

23. Mandela Marketplace website, www.mandelamarketplace.org.

24. Ibid.

25. Mandela Foods Cooperative website, http://www.mandelafoods.com.

26. Author interview with James Bell, December 2015. James is a worker-owner at Mandela Foods Cooperative, December 2015.

27. For more information about the history of Food Not Bombs, see http://foodnotbombs.net/new_site/index.php. Also check out the San Francisco Food Not Bombs chapter at http://www.sffnb.org.

28. To join San Francisco Vegetarian Society and to view a list of current events, see www.sfvs.org.

29. Richie Davis, "Making a Living Wage? Agriculture Justice Project Reaches Out to Area Farmers over Issues of Fairness," *CISA News*, August 20, 2014, http://www.buylocalfood.org/making-a-living-wage-agricultural-justice-project-reaches-out-to-area-farmers-over-issues-of-fairness/.

30. Gosia Wozniacka, "Program Trains Farmworkers to Be Organic Farmers," *Washington Examiner*, December 2, 2012, http://www.washingtonexaminer.com/program-trains-farmworkers-to-be-organic-farmers/article/2514896; Dan Rosen, "ALBA-Agriculture and Land-Based Training Association," *Project: Huertas*, March 12, 2013, https://huertasanth196.wordpress.com/author/huertasanth196/page/2/.

31. A partial list of organizations that prepare and distribute food for needy people can be found in the Appendices.

32. Ban Ki-moon, "Secretary-General's Message for International Day of Cooperatives," July 3, 2010, http://www.un.org/sg/STATEMENTS/index.asp?nid=4664.

# CHAPTER 8
## KEEPING THE VISION

HOW CAN WE harness the enthusiasm for cooperatives while the movement is strong? How can we curb the irresponsible, irrevocable damage caused by global capitalism? How can we address world hunger, climate change, and economic instability? These are hot topics of discussion among co-op supporters. Some scholars predict that the growth of corporate-based income inequality is inevitable.[1] However, other thinkers argue that the apparently inexorable rise of capitalism can be reversed. Two books, *Democracy at Work: A Cure for Capitalism* by Richard Wolff[2] and *America Beyond Capitalism* by Gar Alperovitz,[3] propose alternatives that promote income distribution by sharing sustainable public resources. Both authors argue that true democracy requires actual collaboration among citizens who do more than simply exercise their right to vote.

Organized groups, such as those behind the Arab Spring and the Occupy Movement address the unjust and devastating effects of global corporatism. Food-sector workers are demanding better wages and improved work conditions, and it seems only natural for the co-op movement to expand into this area. Food co-ops have helped to influence social and economic changes in the past, and today's co-ops could certainly broaden their business models to include green sectors, such as wind and solar power, as a way to address current economic disparities and environmental problems.

During the 1970s, other types of co-ops outnumbered food co-ops, but it was the food co-ops that would later sustain the movement. Nonprofit organizations working with food co-ops, food and justice movements, collective households, community gardens, and farmers markets all blossomed. Now, people are reviving a broad-based movement around food, with organizations that address issues of food security and sustainable farming.

Today twenty-first-century co-ops have access to new technologies that allow them to quickly create connections between their members and with other co-ops, as well as with customers, communities, and the public. People are eager to share their expertise, writing business plans and establishing governance tools. We have the lessons of the past to draw from. The question now is: What *more* can be done to sustain the co-op movement, support food co-ops, and address food and justice issues today? We can all take small steps to help our communities; it is these small steps that will lead to a large movement.

## What Can Consumers Do?

By their sheer numbers, consumers are the most vocal body in the food system. We all consume food. We, the consumers, are the driving force of the American economy, and we can wield great influence to determine how food is grown, distributed, and sold. Our food choices, where we buy food, and where that food comes from all have a powerful effect on our health, our local economy, and global issues, including world hunger. Here are some ways you can help strengthen both the local economy and the co-op movement.

- **Educate yourself and others about the benefits of sound food choices.** Teach your children how their food choices affect their future. Whenever possible, buy local, buy organic, buy from co-ops, and ask your affiliated organizations to do the same. Support farm programs, such as CSAs (Community Supported Agriculture programs), that sell shares to support local farms and deliver fresh produce to shareholders. Farmers markets can be a good option for buying fresh produce, with the farmers potentially benefiting from direct sales. Given the growing number of farmers markets, consumers need to be aware of each vendor's relationship with the farmers.
- **Introduce new and sustainable foods and food habits** to your friends and family and share your food with coworkers and neighbors. Remember, food sharing builds community.
- **Go vegetarian, vegan, and healthy!** It has been said that if you eat more beans, more people have beans to eat.

ϩ

Approximately sixteen pounds of grain are required to produce one pound of beef.[4] The increased amount of monocropped soy and corn needed to feed livestock has caused destructive soil erosion.[5] Health-related problems, such as diabetes and heart disease, can be prevented and/or managed with a selective diet that favors fresh fruits and vegetables. According to recent government data, less than a quarter of the U.S. population consumes the amount of fruit and vegetables necessary for a healthy diet.[6] Michael Pollan puts it wisely: "Eat food. Not too much. Mostly plants."[7]

- **Create and support local political platforms** for legislative changes that advocate co-ops, other democratic workplaces, and small farms, and address food and justice issues. Speak up for co-ops and community-building organizations whenever possible.

- **Engage in projects that address local food and justice issues.** Help organizations and institutions that bring fresh foods into food-desert neighborhoods by volunteering and/or lobbying on their behalf. Organize your community and, with the support of local government, establish more farmers markets, food stands, and open bazaars in both urban and rural areas.

- **Promote public education about the many benefits of co-ops.** Online classes about cooperatives are available. In addition, we need required courses about cooperative values and tools in our primary and secondary schools. Ask your local educational institutions to develop these courses.

- **Create more local co-op preschools** like the ones that blossomed in 1960s, when both parents joined the workforce. Co-op schools don't only benefit the children; they also create mutual support among the parents.

- **Encourage local banking and funding institutions to support and invest in cooperatives.** The United Nations recognized the global impact of co-ops in 2012, but financial institutions ignore their value. There are now a few options in the Bay Area for co-ops seeking financial support, including the Northern California Community Loan Fund, but more is still needed. Support microeconomic funding alternatives in your community.

## What Can Farmers Do?

- **Collaborate further with local communities.** Farmers have always worked collectively; they can expand these efforts to include their allied communities. This can include finding new ways to use and distribute products. The farmers partnering with consumers through CSA programs offer a good example of collaboration. In northern California, the Cowgirl Creamery, at Point Reyes Station, and the Strauss Organic Dairy Farm formed a partnership, with Cowgirl making cheese from Strauss's excess organic milk.[8] Some farms collaborate directly with food co-ops to mutual benefit. In the summer of 2015 in Nevada County, California, thirty farms worked together to grow 206 specific produce items specifically for BriarPatch Co-op.[9] That's what cooperation among cooperatives looks like!

- **Educate the public** about issues important to farmers and small farms through farm tours and at farmers markets. An educated public could rise up against "factory farms" and GM foods, gaining clean, non-GMO organics for themselves, while supporting the small farms that grow them.

## What Can Co-ops Do?

- **Honor your organic roots.** Food co-ops advance natural food activism by going organic. When co-ops offer only organic produce, shoppers feel confident about what they're buying, and this can include "grab-and-go" products made on the premises. Demand that deli suppliers use organic ingredients.

- **Buy from and support local farmers, fair-trade vendors, and local entrepreneurs whenever possible.** Buying from local farmers helps to conserve fossil fuels. Purchasing from local wholesalers who support organic farming promotes the future of sustainable agriculture. Support innovative programs like "One Farm at a Time," which conducts campaigns to educate shoppers about a single farmer's financial situation and elicits donations to save a particular farm.[10] Retail food co-ops are an obvious places to find support for such causes.

- **Use environmentally sustainable business options.** Set up a committee to research the many ways in which your co-op can partner with green businesses to find solutions—for example, using solar and wind power. Apply green solutions to everything from minor fixes, like insulation for refrigerator doors, to major changes, for example, installing solar panels. Your co-op will save money, have a positive impact on the environment, and set a great example for others in the community.

◈ **Support food and justice issues through education and selective buying practices.** Carry fair-trade products and educate customers about the far-reaching global impact of choosing them. Support local organizations that advocate around food and justice issues, for example, serving healthy food to the needy. Participate in local events that address issues of food sovereignty and sustainable agriculture. Share healthy food on these occasions; food sharing is a powerful tool for bonding with people.

◈ **Provide co-op education for worker-members.** Making education part of the co-op business model is crucial to co-op survival. It is helpful to educate new applicants about co-op history and the co-op ethos. A "buddy system" could be established during an applicant's training, with an older worker coaching the new worker. This can be especially helpful during periods of high turnover, when new applicants may find themselves struggling with issues that are familiar to experienced workers. Alternately, a series of classes could be set up to discus the "co-op way." Given that we all have a tendency to hold corporate-based values that can sometimes unconsciously clash with co-op goals in unexpected ways, worker co-ops also benefit from an ongoing internal forum for discussing policies and procedures.

◈ **Share leadership.** Leadership is an important skill in a co-op setting. Ideally, experienced workers share leadership roles with new workers, eventually passing the torch. In the 1970s, when task rotation was advocated as a means of maintaining equality among workers, strong leaders were often chastised for being on a "power trip." In contrast, today's cooperators value leadership as an essential business tool, and strive to share, teach, and encourage it whenever possible.

◈ **Teach young people to lead.** The co-op can be a good forum for teaching younger people leadership skills. Today's youth welcome such opportunities. Food co-ops could offer internships to educate the young about the benefits of work-place democracy and about marketing healthy food.

- **Encourage diversity.** It is important that co-ops strive for an even-handed development of leadership among their members. In 1883, in England, Alice Acland started the "women's pages" in the *Cooperative News* weekly to give women a voice in the co-op movement and to expand their role from being merely shoppers—or, "the woman with a basket."[11] Acland later formed the Cooperative Women's Guild to enhance women's role in the cooperative movement. While women and minorities have historically played an important role in building the co-op movement, they have often been denied leadership roles.
- **Create new products and services.** Food co-ops need to think outside of the retail "box." It is possible to pay attention to market competition, without falling in with slick marketing trends. Remember that our original mission is to distribute real food, and there's lots of room for innovation—for example, an organic snack delivery to public schools. Instead of focusing on a one-size-fits-all model, we can tailor our businesses to meet local needs with novel solutions.

    One co-op service that has been missing in the Bay Area since the 1980s is a cooperative warehouse. Both the People's Food System and Berkeley Co-ops stores were successful partially because they could purchase directly from their own warehouses. There are numerous produce suppliers serving Bay Area food co-ops, but today they could still benefit from a one-stop co-op warehouse for other grocery items.

    Bay Area co-ops could also create other social services that focus on co-op values and education, such as child-care centers, youth programs, and summer camps.
- **Educate, connect with, and care for your community.** Co-ops have learned that they must provide excellent service and competitive prices in order to survive. In addition, food co-ops must connect with the larger farm community and with other co-ops. Drawing on their power as an organized force made up of concerned citizens, food co-ops could educate the public about the many benefits the cooperative movement offers. Co-ops could actively engage with the community and learn from the many resources it has to offer.

## What Can the Network of Bay Area Co-op Support Organizations Do?

❖ **Help create new types of co-ops.** Currently, the Bay Area's co-op networks work very hard to encourage co-op growth by assisting new co-ops and by helping small businesses convert to co-ops. At this point, the network should consider extending its reach beyond the retail sector to include other businesses, including warehouse co-ops, homecare co-ops, technology co-ops, housing co-ops, and green energy production co-ops. A large homecare co-op is thriving in New York,[12] and two tech-support co-ops are also doing well in the Bay Area.[13] Nonprofit businesses could also choose to transition into egalitarian, worker-run cooperatives.

❖ **Sponsor more educational events and programs for the public.** The Bay Area's cooperative network plans regular conferences for its members, and maintains lively educational websites where the public can locate a local co-op or read about a co-op event. But the general public would benefit from more co-op events and programs specifically addressing its needs. The co-op network could approach institutions like libraries and schools to organize public forums to educate people about co-ops. For several years, Rainbow Grocery has been hosting an annual Co-op Fair in October that is open to its shoppers. A number of co-ops set up information booths at the event, and various cooperators talk about the benefits of the cooperative business model. Additional events like this could be held in open spaces like Golden Gate Park.

❖ **Help create affordable healthcare, housing, and co-op banks.** These are big issues, requiring large sums of money, but the time has come to tap into the unused resources that create new venues to meet people's needs. Bay Area co-ops have long sought reasonable global healthcare plans for their workers, but other economic issues now need to be addressed. At a time when many co-ops are losing staff because housing in the Bay Area has become unaffordable, old properties could be turned into co-op housing, allowing us to reclaim the San Francisco Bay Area. It would certainly be a dream-come-true to have a "co-op bank," where all workers could share their resources and support one another.

❖ **Collaborate more actively with food and justice organizations** in underserved communities. A good example of this sort of effort is the Democracy at Work Institute's rural development program that helps rural businesses that are on the brink of closing to become worker-owned cooperatives.

A joint event by NoBAWC members in Richmond,
2005. Courtesy of the author's archives.

DAWI cooperates with local economic development agencies to assist them with technical support, including business planning and training for cooperative governance.[15] Projects like these can benefit small local farmers and consumers and create self-sustaining food systems.

> *"Economically, the [co-op] sector could be incredibly powerful if we link up with other cooperative sectors—agriculture, consumer co-ops, housing co-ops, producer co-ops. . . . I have a vision that we can quite adequately meet people's needs through cooperatives."*[14]
> —*Melissa Hoover, executive director of the Democracy at Work Institute (DAWI)*

## What Can Government Do?

❖ **Support co-ops with financial incentives and pro-co-op legislation.** In many European and Asian countries, local and federal governments encourage cooperatives with monetary and legislative support. In the United States, government incentives (such as tax breaks for co-ops) would be welcome and justified, given that co-ops distribute their surplus to their members, thus benefiting the local economy.

❖ **In 2015, the City of New York acknowledged the important economic role that co-ops play** when it designated $1.2 million for worker-owned co-op development.[16] The San Francisco Bay Area's local governments could emulate this action by providing financial incentives for the establishment of cooperatives, particularly food and housing co-ops. This could, at the same time, provide a positive way to develop the vacant lots in underserved neighborhoods. Struggling and failing businesses could be encouraged to convert to cooperatives with local government support. The Bay Area's very active co-op network and cooperators are here, just waiting to start new co-ops!

❖ **Local governments could also encourage financial institutions**, such as credit unions and banks, to establish specific loan programs to help cooperatives. In return, co-op workers would support these lenders by banking with these establishments.

Community Garden near Alemany Farmers Market, 2015. Photo by Rezz Sacharoff.

- ❖ **Teach sustainable food systems and cooperative business models in public schools.** Public education could do much to raise awareness about the inequities in our food system. Classes on health and fitness are increasingly available in schools and universities; these classes should address the importance of ensuring access to healthy food for everyone. Classes in business, law, sociology, and agriculture should include information about our food systems and cooperative business models. This knowledge would allow citizens to take action to guarantee food sustainability and better public health.
- ❖ **To educate the youth regarding sustainable food systems,** the EcoSF Farm program was founded in 2010, with the support of two San Francisco public high schools, the Academy of Arts and Sciences and the School of the Arts.

EcoSF, a non-profit organization run by a cooperative team of three educators, set up a farm/garden that "provides [students] ecological education, the science of relationships and . . . helps the community better understand the local environment . . . [and] the intricate web of life through cooperation, not domination."[17] Witness here a new generation of cooperators working to find solutions that will support the future economy of San Francisco!

Momentum is building to pool the energy of the small but significant number of people who care about reclaiming our food system. If we were to effectively organize all of our many resources in our communities and co-ops and among consumers and our government allies, there could be substantial co-op growth in the United States. If food co-ops become an established part of mainstream commerce, we might begin to see fresh organic produce in every market—with only a few commercial products on the side! If farmers, farmworkers, food sector workers, consumers, and students were to unite in large numbers and act together to make our food system sustainable, then the agro-conglomerates could surely be taken down, and food could truly be distributed "For People, Not for Profit." As Margaret Mead once said: "Never doubt that a small group of thoughtful, committed citizens can change the world. Indeed, it is the only thing that ever has."[18]

## Notes

1.  Thomas Piketty, *Capital in the Twenty-First Century*, trans. Arthur Goldhammer (Cambridge, MA: Belknap Press, 2014).
2.  Richard Wolff, *Democracy at Work: A Cure for Capitalism* (Chicago: Haymarket Books, 2012).
3.  Gar Alperovitz, *America Beyond Capitalism, Reclaiming our Wealth, Our Liberty, and Our Democracy* (Boston: Democracy Collaborative Press, 2011).
4.  John Robbins, *Diet for a New America* (New Hampshire: Still Point Publishing, 1987), 351.
5.  Frances Moore Lappé, *Diet for a Small Planet*, 20th anniversary edition (New York: Ballantine Books, 1991), 79–81.
6.  "Center for Disease Control and Prevention, Morbidity and Mortality Report (MMWR): Specific Trends in Fruit and Vegetable Consumption among Adults—United States 2000–2009," September 10, 2010, http://www.cdc.gov, vol. 59: no. 35.
7.  Michael Pollan, *In Defense of Food: An Eater's Manifesto* (New York: Penguin Group, 2008).

8.   "The Cowgirl Story," https://www.cowgirlcreamery.com/
     the-cowgirl-story.
9.   "Season premiere: 30 local farms, 206 vegetables and fruits,"
     *The Vine*, June–July 2015, http://www.briarpatch.coop/
     season-premiere-30-local-farms-206-vegetables-and-fruits/.
10.  One Farm at a Time, see http://www.community.coop/onefarmatatime.
11.  Catherine Webb, *The Woman with the Basket: The History of the
     Women's Co-operative Guild 1883–1927* (Manchester: Cooperative
     Wholesale Society's Printing Works, 1927).
12.  Cooperative Homecare Associates (CHCA), http://www.icsny.org.
13.  Electric Embers, an internet hosting service, see http://www.
     electricembers.coop, and Tech Collective, a tech support and IT
     consulting firm, see http://www.techcollective.com.
14.  "Worker Owned Cooperatives," *Business Matters*, January 15, 2010,
     http://businessmatters.net/2010/01/worker-owned-cooperatives/.
     Melissa Hoover, executive director of U.S. Federation of Worker
     Cooperative, interviewed by Thomas White.
15.  "Rural Development," Democracy at Work Institute, http://institute.
     usworker.coop/projects/rural-Development.
16.  Liz Pleasant, "Worker-Owned Co-ops Get $1
     Million in NYC Spending," *Yes! Magazine*, June 27,
     2014, http://www.yesmagazine.org/commonomics/
     worker-owned-co-ops-get-one-million-dollars-in-new-york-budget.
17.  For the mission statement of EcoSF Farm, see http://eco-sf.org.
18.  Frequently Asked Questions About Mead/Batson," Institute for
     Intercultural Studies, http://www.interculturalstudies.org/faq.
     html#quote.

# APPENDICES

# SUGGESTED LITERATURE AND OTHER RESOURCES FOR FURTHER STUDY

## Books on Co-ops, Co-op History, and Tool Boxes

Abrams, John. *The Company We Keep: Reinventing Small Business for People, Community and Place.* White River Junction, VT: Chelsea Green Publishing, 2005.

Adams, Frank T. *Putting Democracy to Work: A Practical Guide for Starting and Managing Worker-Owned Businesses,* 2nd edition. San Francisco: Berrett-Koehler Publishers, 1993.

Baldwin, Van P. *Legal Sourcebook for California Cooperatives: A Legal Guide for Cooperatives Incorporating and Operating under the California Consumer Cooperative Corporation Law,* 3rd edition. Davis, CA: Center for Cooperatives, University of California, 2004. Electronic format (PDF).

Carlsson, Chris, and Lisa Ruth Elliott, eds. *Ten Years That Shook the City: San Francisco, 1968–1978.* San Francisco: City Lights Publications, 2011. (Has a chapter on PFS.)

Cheese Board Collective. *The Cheese Board: Collective Works.* Berkeley: Ten Speed Press, 2003.

Coontz, E. Kim. *Bringing Families Together: A Guide to Parent Cooperatives.* Davis, CA: Center for Cooperatives, University of California, 1992.

Hansen, Gary B., E. Kim Coontz, and Audrey Malan. *Steps to Starting a Worker Co-op: A Legal Sourcebook for California Cooperatives.* Davis, CA: Center for Cooperatives Library, University of California, 1997; co-published with the Northwest Cooperative Federation, 1999. Original printed format and electronic PDF format.

Honigsberg, Peter Jan, Bernard Kamoroff, and Jim Beatty. *We Own It: Starting and Managing Cooperatives and Employee-Owned Ventures*, revised edition. Bell Springs Publishing, 1991. (Out of print but often available via internet sources.)

Lund, Margaret, and the North Country Cooperative Development Foundation. *In Good Company: The Guide to Cooperative Employee Ownership: A Worker Cooperative Tool Box*. Minneapolis: North Country Cooperative Foundation, 2006.

Mcad, Margaret, ed. *Cooperation and Competition among Primitive Peoples*. Gloucester, MA: Peter Smith, 1976.

Nembhard, Jessica Gordon. *Collective Courage: A History of African American Cooperative Economic Thought and Practice*. University Park, PA: Penn State University Press, 2014.

Northcountry Cooperative Foundation. *Worker Cooperative Toolbox: In Good Company—The Guide to Employee Ownership*. Minneapolis: Northcountry Cooperative Foundation, 2006. Electronic PDF format.

Vannucci, Delfina, and Richard Singer. *Come Hell or High Water: A Handbook on Collective Process Gone Awry*. Oakland, CA: AK Press, 2013.

Wright, Chris. *Worker Cooperatives and Revolution: History and Possibilities in the United States*. Bradenton, FL: BookLocker.com, 2014.

## Books on Socioeconomic Change via Co-ops and Other Community-Based Economies

Allard, Jenna, Carl Davidson, and Julie Matthaei eds. *Solidarity Economy: Building Economy for People and Planet*. Chicago: ChangeMaker Publications, 2008.

Benello, C. George. *From the Ground Up: Essays on Grassroots and Workplace Democracy*. Edited by Len Krimerman, Frank Lindenfeld, Carol Korty, and Julian Benello. Boston: South End Press, 1992.

Cavanagh, John, and Jerry Mander, eds. *Alternatives to Economic Globalization: A Better World Is Possible*, 2nd edition. San Francisco: Berrett-Koehler Publishers, 2004.

Cornwell, Janelle, Michael Johnson, and Adam Trott, with Julie Graham. *Building Co-operative Power: Stories and Strategies from*

*Worker Co-operatives in the Connecticut River Valley.* Amherst, MA: Levellers Press, 2013.

Hightower, Jim, with Susan DeMarco. *Swim against the Current: Even a Dead Fish Can Go with the Flow.* New Jersey: John Wiley & Sons, 2008.

Korten, David. *The Post-Corporate World: Life after Capitalism.* San Francisco: Berrett-Koehler Publishers, 1999.

Lappé, Frances Moore. *EcoMind: Changing the Way We Think to Create a World We Want.* New York: Nation Books Division of Perseus Books, 2013.

Nadeau, E.G. *The Cooperative Solution: How the United States Can Tame Recessions, Reduce Inequality and Protect the Environment.* Createspace, 2012.

Restakis, John. *Humanizing the Economy: Co-operatives in the Age of Capital.* British Columbia, Canada: New Society Publishers, 2010.

## Books on Vegetarian Lifestyle, Cooking, and Nutrition

Lappé, Frances Moore. *Diet for a Small Planet,* 20th anniversary edition. New York: Ballantine Books, 1991.

Robbins, John. *Diet for a New America.* New York: Still Point Publishing, 1987.

Robertson, Laurel, Carol Flinders, and Brian Ruppenthal. *Laurel's Kitchen: A Handbook for Vegetarian Cookery and Nutrition.* Berkeley, CA: Ten Speed Press, 1986.

Sacharoff, Shanta Nimbark, *Flavors of India,* revised edition. Summertown, TN: Book Publishing Company, 1996.

_____. *Ethnic Vegetarian Kitchen: Recipes with Guidelines for Nutrition.* San Francisco: 101 Production, 1984. (Out of print but available through online book dealers.)

_____. Recipes in cooking column in *India Currents,* San Jose, CA. www.indiacurrents.com.

## Magazines/Newsletters on Food Co-ops, Food, and Justice Issues

*Cooperative Grocer Magazine*: www.grocer.coop.
*Earth Island Journal*: www.earthisland.org
*Edible San Francisco*: www.ediblesanfrancisco.ediblefeast.com.

*GEO*; Grassroots Economic Organizing: www.geo.coop for archives
*Mother Jones*: www.motherjones.com.
*Rural Cooperative Magazine*: www.extension.org.
*Yes! Magazine*: www.yesmagazine.org.

## Films and Videos on Co-ops and Co-op History

*Beyond the Bottom Line: American Worker Cooperatives*. A half-hour
documentary made for public television about various work-
er-owned co-ops in the United States. Produced by Headlamp
Pictures, 2013. Visit http://headlamppictures.com/worker-coops.
*Democracy in the Workplace: Three Worker-Owned Businesses in
Action:* A focus on three cooperatives: Cheeseboard, Rainbow,
and Inkworks Press. By Robert Purdy and Margot Smith. Berkeley,
CA: Off Center Video, 1999.
*Developing a Budget for Creating a Food Cooperative: A Workshop by
Stuart Reid at the California Cooperative Conference in Oakland,
California, May 2012.* Film by Jai Jai Noire. Produced by Mighty Small
Films. Visit http://www.mightysmallfilms.com or contact Jai Jai at
(510) 531-5373.
*Food for Change.* A feature-length documentary on food co-ops as a
vehicle for social change in American culture. Directed by Steve
Alves, 2015. Visit http://www.foodforchange.coop. For more in-
formation, contact Michael@foodforchanges.coop.
*The Mondragon Experiment:* Parts 1 and 2. A BBC documentary about
co-ops in Spain's Basque region.
Other Avenues has produced two films. Visit http://otheravenues.
coop or http://www.youtube.com/user/JJNoire.
*Shift Change.* A documentary film about worker-owned enterprises
in North America and in Mondragon, Spain. Made by Melissa
Young and Mark Dworkin. Produced by Moving Images, 2012.
Visit http://www.bulfrogfilms.com info@bullfrogfilms.com.
*This Way Out: A Guide to Starting a Worker Cooperative.* By Jai Jai
Noire. Produced by Mighty Small Films. Visit http://www.migh-
tysmallfilms.com or contact Jai Jai at (510) 531-5373.

# LISTS OF CO-OPS, MARKETS, AND ORGANIZATIONS

## Retail Food Co-op Markets in the San Francisco Bay Area

**Berkeley Student Food Collective**
2440 Bancroft Way, #102, Berkeley, CA 94704
(510) 845-1985 •membership@foodcollective.org
www.berkeleystudentfoodcollective.org

**Davis Food Co-op**
620 G Street, Davis, CA 94608
(530) 758-2667 • dwalter@davisfood.coop
www.davisfood.coop

**Kresge Food Co-op**
1156 High Street, Santa Cruz, CA 95064
(831) 426-1506 • kresge.ucsc.edu/activities/coops/food-coop.html

**Mandela Foods Cooperative**
1430 7th Street, Oakland, CA 94607
(510) 452-1133 • www.mandelafood.com

**Other Avenues**
3930 Judah Street, San Francisco, CA 94122
(415) 661-7475 • info@otheravenues.coop
www.otheravenues.coop

**Rainbow Grocery Co-op**
1745 Folsom Street, San Francisco, CA 94103
(415) 863-0620 • comments@rainbowgrocery.coop
www.rainbow.coop

**Sacramento Natural Foods Co-op**
1900 Alhambra Boulevard, Sacramento, CA 95816
(916) 455-2667 • comments@sacfoodcoop.com
www.sacfoodcoop.com

## Retail Food Co-op Markets in California

**(List created by the California Center for Cooperative Development, 2014. Updated by Shanta Nimbark Sacharoff, 2016)**

### Established Food Co-ops:

1. North Coast Co-op, Eureka
2. North Coast Co-op, Arcata
3. Chico Natural Foods Cooperative, Chico
4. Ukiah Natural Foods Co-op, Ukiah
5. Quincy Natural Foods Co-op, Quincy
6. BriarPatch Co-op, Grass Valley
7. Sacramento Natural Foods Co-op, Sacramento
8. San Luis Obispo (SLO) Natural Foods Co-op, San Luis Obispo
9. Isla Vista Food Cooperative, Isla Vista
10. Co-opportunity Natural Foods, Santa Monica
11. Ocean Beach People's Organic Food Market, San Diego
12. Davis Food Co-op, Davis
13. Other Avenues, San Francisco
14. Rainbow Grocery Co-op, San Francisco
15. Kresge Food Co-op, Santa Cruz

### New Food Cooperatives (2008 to 2013):

16. Arena Market and Cafe, Point Arena
17. Berkeley Student Food Cooperative, Berkeley
18. Placerville Natural Food Cooperative, Placerville
19. Mandela Foods Cooperative, Oakland
20. Feather River Food Co-op, Portola (Quincy Natural Foods' second store)

### Food Co-ops in the Planning Stage

21. Ojai Food Cooperative, Ojai
22. Paso Food Co-op, Paso Robles
23. SoLA Food Co-op, South Los Angeles
24. Riverside Food Co-op, Riverside
25. San Clemente Community Market, San Clemente

# Retail Food Co-op Markets Map

Sacramento

Los Angeles

San Diego

## Selected Farmers Markets and Farm Stands in the San Francisco Bay Area

There are many farmers markets in San Francisco Bay Area. New markets spring up, some of the old ones close, others thrive. Some are seasonal, others are open all year round, a day or two week. Listed below are the farmers markets that are open all year round, on designated days. For an updated list of San Francisco Bay Area farmers markets and their current hours of operation, contact Pacific Coast Farmers' Market Association, 5060 Commercial Circle, Suite A, Concord, CA 94520. Phone: (800) 949-FARM. Or check out individual markets at their locations.

### San Francisco

**Alemany Farmers Market**
Corner of Bayshore and Putnam
**Crocker Galleria Farmers Market**
50 Post Street at Montgomery
**Ferry Plaza Certified Farmers Market**
Corner of Embarcadero and Green Street
**Fillmore Farmers Market**
O'Farrell and Fillmore
**Fort Mason Farmers Market**
Marina and Buchanan
**Heart of the City**
Corner of Market and Seventh Streets, near the Main Public Library
**Clement Street/Inner Richmond Farmers Market**
Clement Street, between Second and Fourth Avenues
**Sunset Farmers Market**
Eighth Avenue and Judah Street
**Mercado Comunitario De La Mission**
Bartlett Street at 22nd Street
**Noe Valley Farmers Market**
Vicksburg and Sanchez Streets
**Stonestown Farmers Market**
Buckingham Way, near 19th Avenue
**Tenderloin/ Fern Alley Farmers Market**
55 Fern Street

### Berkeley

**Berkeley Certified Farmers Market**
Derby and Martin Luther King Way

**Farm Fresh Choice Farms at the following locations:**
- Bahia Child Care Center, 1718 Eighth Street (at Virginia)
- Berkeley Youth Alternatives, 1255 Allston Way (at Bonar)
- Young Adult Project, 1730 Oregon Street (at Martin Luther King Jr.)
- Frances Albrier Community Center in San Pablo Park, 2800 Park Street (at Oregon)

## Oakland
**Jack London Square Farmers Market**
Jack London Square, Broadway and Embarcadero
Website: www.cuesa.org/markets/jack-london-square-farmers-market
**Mandela Farmers Market**
Seventh and Mandela Streets, West Oakland
**Mobile Market (run by the People's Grocery)**
820 Wood St.
Phone: (510) 763-0328
Website: www.peoplesgrocery.org/
**Old Oakland Certified Farmers Market**
Location: 9th and Broadway

## Richmond
**Farm Fresh Choice Farms at the following locations:**
- Kaiser Permanente Richmond Medical Center, 901 Nevin Avenue (at Harbor Way)
- Missionary Baptist Church parking lot, 1427 Filbert Street (at Gertrude)

## Marin County
Sunday Marin Farmers Market, Marin Civic Center, San Rafael

## Farmers/Producers/Consumers Outreach in California
**Community Supported Agriculture (CSA):**
www.csasanfrancisco.com
**Agriculture & Land-Based Training Association (ALBA):**
www.albafarmers.org
**Bay Area Seed Interchange Library (BASIL):**
www.ecologycenter.org/basil
**California Certified Organic Farmers (CCOF):**
www.ccof.org
**Community Alliance with Family Farms (CAFF):**
www.caff.org/

## Short List of Organizations That Feed the Hungry in the Bay Area

(Note: The days of meals served may change and services may close without notice.)

| Organization | When | Where they serve |
|---|---|---|
| Curry Without Worry | Tues. 5:30PM | Civic Center Plaza, Downtown S.F. Near Public Library (Fulton & Hyde) |
| Food Not Bombs | Thurs. 7PM | Near 16th Street Bart Station Mission & 16th Streets, San Francisco |
| Glide Memorial Church | Every day Breakfast: 8:00AM Lunch: Noon | 330 Ellis at Taylor Downtown San Francisco |
| Martin de Porres House of Hospitality | Every day Breakfast and/or Lunch | 225 Potrero (near 16th Street) Potrero District, San Francisco |
| St. Vincent De Paul Society | Tues. through Sat. from 10:45AM to 12:45PM | 675 23rd Street, Oakland |

## Food and Justice Organizations in the San Francisco Bay Area

*Listed below are some organizations that work on food and justice issues in local communities in the San Francisco Bar Area*

Center for Urban Education about Sustainable Agriculture (CUESA).
    webmaster@cuesa.org • info@cuesa.org

The Ecology Center. www.ecologycenter.org

Farms to Grow, Inc. www.farmstogrow.com

Food First. www.foodfirst.org

Hunters Point Family. www.hunterspointfamily.org/our-approach/
    healthy-lifestyles/

Oakland Food Policy Council. info@oaklandfood.org

Planting Justice. www.plantingjustice.org

Veggielution Community Farm. www.veggielution.org

## Network of Bay Area's Worker Cooperatives (NoBAWC) List

This list (updated 2015) includes Arizmendi Association, Cheese Board, Pizza Board, and Arizmendi bakeries. Many of the worker cooperatives listed here are not currently paying members of NoBAWC.

To promote all worker-owned cooperatives, NoBAWC has included as many as possible. New worker-owned co-ops should notify NoBAWC.

**ACCI Gallery**
1652 Shattuck Avenue, Berkeley, CA 94709
(510) 843-2527 • http://www.accigallery.com/

**Adobe Books & Art Cooperative**
3130 24th Street, San Francisco, CA 94110
(415) 864-3936 • www.adobebooks.com/

**Alchemy Café**
1741 Alcatraz Avenue, Berkeley, CA 94703
(530) 680-8874 • eventsatalchemycafe@gmail.com

**ARIZMENDI BAKERIES**

**Arizmendi Emeryville**
4301 San Pablo Avenue, Emeryville, CA 94608
(510) 547-0550 • www.arizmendi-bakery.org

**Arizmendi Oakland**
3265 Lakeshore Avenue, Oakland, CA 94610
(510) 268-8849 • arizmendilakeshore.com

**Arizmendi San Francisco (Sunset District)**
1331 9th Avenue, San Francisco, CA 94122
(415) 566-3117 • www.arizmendibakery.com

**Arizmendi San Francisco (Mission District)**
1268 Valencia Street, San Francisco, CA 94110
(415) 826-9218 • arizmendi-valencia.squarespace.com

**Arizmendi San Rafael**
1002 Fourth Street, San Rafael, CA 94901
(415) 456-4093 • www.arizmendi-sanrafael.coop

**Arizmendi Association of Cooperatives.**
1904 Franklin Street #204, Oakland, CA 94612
(415) 683-3335 • www.arizmendi.coop

**Bay Area Health Collective (BAHC)**
3150 18th Street, San Francisco CA 94102
(415) 800 -8790 • www.bayareahealthcollective.org

**Berkeley Free Clinic**
2339 Durant Avenue, Berkeley, CA 94704
(800) 625-4642 • www.berkeleyfreeclinic.org

**Bike Kitchen**
650H Florida Street, San Francisco, CA 94110
(415) 647-2453 • www.bikekitchen.org

**BioFuel Oasis**
1441 Ashby Avenue, Berkeley, CA 94702
(510) 665-5509 • www.biofueloasis.com

**Bound Together Bookstore**
1369 Haight Street, San Francisco, CA 94117
(415) 431-8355 • www.boundtogetherbooks.wordpress.com

**Box Dog Bikes**
494 14th Street, San Francisco, CA 94103
(415) 431-9627 • www.boxdogbikes.com

**Cheese Board**
1504 Shattuck Avenue, Berkeley, CA 94709
(510) 549-3183 • www.cheeseboardcollective.coop

**Cheese Board Pizza**
1512 Shattuck Avenue, Berkeley, CA 94709
(510) 549-3055 • www.cheeseboardcollective.coop

**CoFed (Cooperative Food Empowerment Directive)**
2323 Broadway, #22, Oakland, CA 94612
www.cofed.coop

**Cricket Courier Cooperative**
268 Bush Street #3238, San Francisco, CA 94104
(415) 850-9193 • www.cricketcourier.com

**Cupid Courier Collective**
150 Sutter Street #313, San Francisco, CA 94104
www.cupidcourier.com

**Design Action Collective**
1730 Franklin Street #103, Oakland, CA 94612
(510) 452-1912
www.designaction.org

**DIG Cooperative**
5410 Dover Street, Oakland, CA 94609
(510) 316-3620 • www.dig.coop

**Ecology Center of San Francisco**
555 Portola Drive, San Francisco, CA 94131
(415) 290-6763 • www.eco-sf.org

**Electric Embers Cooperative, Inc.**
733 Page Street, San Francisco, CA 94117
(800) 843-6197 • www.electricembers.coop

**Emma's Eco-Clean**
1155 Broadway #129, Redwood City, CA 94063
(650) 261-1788 • www.emmasecoclean.com

**Energy Solidarity Cooperative**
55 Harrison Street # 300, Oakland, CA 94607
www.energy-coop.com

**Fusion Latina**
PO Box 2833, Richmond, CA 94801
(510) 730-6072 • www.facebook.com/Fusion-Latina-Collective-Catering-
    Service-448343688569540/

**Heartwood Cooperative Woodshop**
2547 8th Street #27, Berkeley, CA 94710
(510) 845-4887 • www.heartwoodshop.net

**Home Green Home**
2301 Mission Street #201B, San Francisco, CA 94110
(415) 285-5525 • www.homegreenhomesf.com

**Juice Bar Collective**
2114 Vine Street, Berkeley, CA 94709
(510) 548-8473 • www.juicebarcollective.com

**Mandela Foods Cooperative**
1430 7th Street, Oakland, CA 94607
(510) 452-1133 • www.mandelafoods.com/

**Missing Link Bicycle Cooperative**
1988 Shattuck Avenue, Berkeley, CA 94704
(510) 843-7471 • www.missinglink.org.

**Modern Times Bookstore**
2919 24th Street, San Francisco, CA 94110
(415) 282-9246 • www.moderntimesbookstore.com

**Nanofarms Cooperative**
1425 Bay Road, East Palo Alto, CA 94303
(650) 817-8801 • www.nanofarms.com

**Natural Home Cleaning Professionals**
3228 Fruitvale Avenue, Oakland, CA 94602
(510) 878-9423 • www.naturalhomecleaning.com

**924 Gilman Street**
924 Gilman Street, Berkeley, CA 94710
(510) 525-9926 • www.924gilman.org

**Omni Commons**
4799 Shattuck Avenue, Oakland, CA 94609
www.omnicommons.org

**Other Avenues**
3930 Judah Street, San Francisco, CA 9412
(415) 661-7475 • www.otheravenues.coop

**Pedal Express**
PO Box 10141, Berkeley, CA 94710
(510) 843-7339 • www.pedalexpress.com

**Radical Designs Cooperative**
1201 Martin Luther King Jr. Way, Suite 200, Oakland, CA 94612
(415) 738-0456 • www.radicaldesigns.org

**Rainbow Grocery Cooperative**
1745 Folsom Street, San Francisco, CA 94103
(415) 863-0620 • www.rainbow.coop

**Rhizome Urban Garden Cooperative**
16 Sherman Street, San Francisco, CA 94103
(415) 724-2615 or (850) 376-0820 • www.rhizomegardens.com

**San Francisco Community Land Trust**
PO Box 420982, San Francisco, CA 94142
(415) 399-1490 • www.sfclt.org

**San Francisco Green Cab**
2940 16th Street #313, San Francisco, CA 94111
(415) 626-4733 • www.greencabsf.com

**San Francisco Mime Troupe**
855 Treat Street, San Francisco, CA 94110
(415) 285-1717 • www.sfmt.org

**San Francisco Steiner Free School Time Bank**
1743 Golden Gate Avenue Apt. # 7, San Francisco, CA 94115
(415) 590-7276 • community.timebanks.org/timebanks/san-francisco-
    steiner-free-school-time-bank

**Small Multiples**
195 41st Street # 11215, Oakland, CA 94611
(510) 545-9235 • www.smallmultiples.coop

**Suigetsukan Martial Arts School**
103 International Boulevard, Oakland, CA 94606
(510) 452-3941 • www.suigetsukan.org

**Taste of Denmark Bakery**
3401 Telegraph Avenue, Oakland, CA 94609
(510) 422-8889 • www.tastedenmark.com

**TeamWorks Cleaning**
1159 Sonora Court, Sunnyvale, CA 94086
(650) 940-9773 • www.teamworks.coop

**TeamWorks Sustainable Landscapes**
1159 Sonora Court, Sunnyvale, CA 94086
(408) 250-8619 • www.teamworks.coop

**TechCollective**
263 San Carlos St., San Francisco, CA 94110
(415) 285-8882 • www.techcollective.com

**Three Stone Hearth Cooperative**
1581 University Ave, Berkeley, CA 94703
(510) 981-1334 • www.threestonehearth.com/

## Partial List of Co-op Support Organizations: Local, National, and International

**Arizmendi Association**
1904 Franklin Street, Suite 204 Oakland, CA 94612
aac@arizmendi.coop • (415) 683-3335 Fax: (510) 858-5334
www.arizmendi.coop

**California Center for Cooperative Development (CCCD)**
979 F Street, Suite A-1, Davis, CA 95616
info@cccd.coop • 530-297-1032
www.cccd.coop/

**Democracy at Work Institute (DAWI)**
1904 Franklin Street, Ste. 400, Oakland, CA 94612
info@institute.usworker.coop • (415) 379-9201
www.institute.coop

**Grassroots Economic Organizing (GEO)**
www.geonewsletter.org

**International Cooperative Alliance (ICA)**
Avenue Milcamps 105, 1030 Brussels, Belgium

ica@ica.coop • +32 (2) 743 10 30
www.ica.coop

**National Cooperative Business Association (NCBA)**
1401 New York Avenue NW, Suite 1100, Washington, DC 20005
jtorres@ncba.coop • (202) 638-6222 Fax: (202) 638-1374
www.ncba.coop/

**National Co+op Grocers (NCG)**
Formerly known as National Co-op Grocers Association (NCGA)
14 S. Linn Street, Iowa City, Iowa, 52240
(866) 709-2667 or (612) 424-7545
www.ncg.coop

**Network of Bay Area Cooperatives (NoBAWC)**
NoBAWC, PO Box 3246, Oakland, CA 94609
info@nobawc.org • (510) 736-2667
www.nobawc.org/

**US Federation of Worker Cooperatives (USFWC)**
1904 Franklin Street, Suite 400, Oakland, CA 94612
info@usworker.coop • (415) 392-7277
www.usworker.coop/

**University of Wisconsin Center for Cooperatives**
427 Lorch Street, Madison, WI 53706
info@uwcc.wisc,edu • (608) 262-3981
www.uwcc.wisc.edu

# BIBLIOGRAPHY

**Books on Co-ops, Co-op History, and
Tool Boxes Used in This Book**

Alperovitz, Gar. *America Beyond Capitalism: Reclaiming Our Wealth, Our Liberty, and Our Democracy*. Takoma Park: Democracy Collaborative Press, 2011.

Conkin, Paul K. *Tomorrow a New World: The New Deal Community Program*. Ithaca: Cornell University Press, 1959.

Cox, Craig. *Storefront Revolution*. New Brunswick, NJ: Rutgers University Press, 1994.

Curl, John. *For All the People: Uncovering the Hidden History of Cooperation, Cooperative Movements, and Communalism in America*, 2nd edition. Oakland, CA: PM Press, 2012.

Fullerton, Michael, ed. *What Happened to the Berkeley Co-op? A Collection of Opinions*. Davis, CA: Center for Cooperatives, University of California, 1992.

Lappé, Frances Moore. *Diet for a Small Planet*, 20th anniversary edition. New York: Ballantine Books, 1991.

Lyons, Oren, and John Mohawk, eds. *Exiled in the Land of the Free: Democracy, Indian Nations and the U.S. Constitution*. Santa Fe, NM: Clear Light Publishers, 1992.

McLuhan, Marshall. *The Gutenberg Galaxy: The Making of Typographic Man*. Toronto: University of Toronto Press, 1962.

_____. *Understanding Media: The Extensions of Man*. New York: McGraw-Hill, 1964.

Mead, Margaret, ed. *Cooperation and Competition among Primitive Peoples*. Gloucester, MA: Pewter Smith, 1976.

Parker, Florence. *The First 125 Years: The History of Distributive Service Cooperation in the United States, 1829–1954*. Chicago: Cooperative League of the USA, 1956.

Patel, Raj. *Stuffed and Starved: The Hidden Battle for the World Food System*, revised edition. Brooklyn, NY: Melville House Publishing, 2012.

Piketty, Thomas. *Capital in the Twenty-First Century*. Translated by Arthur Goldhammer. Massachusetts: Belknap Press, 2014.

Pollan, Michael. *In Defense of Food: An Eater's Manifesto*. New York: Penguin Group, 2008.

Robbins, John. *Diet for a New America*. New York: Still Point Publishing, 1987.

Ronco, William. *Food Co-ops: An Alternative to Shopping in Supermarkets*. Boston: Beacon Press, 1974.

Roy, Ewell P. *Cooperatives: Development, Principles, and Management*, 3rd edition. Danville, IL: Interstate Printers and Publishers, 1976.

Sacharoff, Shanta Nimbark. *Flavors of India*. Summertown, TN: Book Publishing Company, 1996.

_____. *The Ethnic Vegetarian Kitchen*. San Francisco: 101 Productions (Distributed by Ortho Information, San Ramon, CA).

Wickstrom, Lois. *The Food Conspiracy Cookbook*. San Francisco: 101 Productions, 1974.

Wolff, Richard. *Democracy at Work: A Cure for Capitalism*. Chicago: Haymarket Books, 2012.

Zeuli, Kimberley A., and Robert Cropp. *Cooperatives: Principles and Practices in the 21st Century*. Madison: University of Wisconsin, Center for Cooperatives, 2007.

Zinn, Howard. *The Indispensible Zinn: The Essential Writings of the "People's Historian."* Edited by Timothy Patrick McCarthy. New York: The New Press, 2012.

## Periodicals, Newsletters, and Other Media Publications Used in This Book

*Berkeley Barb*, a weekly underground newspaper published from 1965 to 1985 in Berkeley, California, focused on the many countercultural political topics of that era. For archives, visit: http://www.berkeleybarb.net or http://chroniclingamerica.loc.gov/lccn/sn78001858.

*Collective Action*, a newsletter of NoBAWC (network of Bay Area Worker Cooperatives). For archives, http://nobawc.org/newsletter-archives-2/.

Democracy at Work Institute 2015 Press Kit: Authors: Democracy at Work Institute and United States Federation of Worker Cooperatives Staff: 2014–15; http://institute.coop/news/democracy-work-instituteusfwc-press-kit.

*Food for Change*, a feature-length documentary on food co-ops as a vehicle for social change in American culture, directed by Steve Alves. To view, visit http://www.foodforchange.coop. For a copy of the film, contact Michael@foodforchanges.coop.

Grassroots Economic Organizing (GEO), a group of activists working together to promote an economy based on democratic participation, worker and community ownership, social and economic justice, and ecological sustainability through movement-building and connecting thorough the online publication, *GEO*. For archives, visit http://www.geo.coop.

*India Currents*, a monthly magazine by the Indian American Community based in the Bay Area (a good magazine to find Indian Vegetarian recipes).

"The Upshot," *New York Times*: http://www.nytimes.com/section/upshot/.

*Other Ave-News*, a newsletter of Other Avenues Food Store, 3930 Judah Street, San Francisco, CA. http://www.otheravenues.coop.

*Storefront Extension*, newsletter of the People's Food System, 1974–75. Archives are kept in the local history section of the San Francisco Public Library.

*Turnover*, newspaper/magazine of the People's Food System published as a continuation of *Storefront Extension*. Archives are kept in the local history section of the San Francisco Public Library.

*USFWC NEWS*, a biannual newsletter of the United States Federation of Worker Cooperatives: usworker.coop.

*The Vine*, BriarPatch Co-op's community newsletter: http://www.briarpatch.coop/know-briarpatch/the-vine-newsletter.

# ACKNOWLEDGMENTS

MANY COOPERATORS HELPED me to collect material for this book by giving me interviews, making suggestions, and providing photos and artwork. You will find some of their names in endnotes and quotes, but many more folks helped me with the creation of this book. I wish to thank them all for their valuable assistance. My special thanks to my coworkers at Other Avenues who asked me to, someday, write this all down. Here it is.

In addition, I want to thank my two editors, Beth Levitan and Lorri Ungaretti, who helped me shape and organize the book and PM Press's staff members who put on the final touches.

Many thanks to my two friends Dorothy Fellner and Dennis Bournique who have been with me since the Food Conspiracy days and continue to help the food co-op community.

Many thanks to my family: my husband, Rick Sugarek, for his patience during the years it took me to write the book; my children Serena and Sanjay, for their emotional support; and my son Reyaz (Rezz), who took some photos and accompanied me to visit some co-ops.

Many cooperators built the food co-op network in the San Francisco Bay Area before I started and many worked with me and many more will continue to create and participate in more co-ops. I wish to thank us all for making other avenues possible.

# INDEX

Page numbers in *italic* refer to illustrations. "Passim" (literally "scattered") indicates intermittent discussion of a topic over a cluster of pages.

of Berkeley (CCB); Ma Revolution; University of California, Berkeley

*Berkeley Barb*, 47

Berkeley Cooperative Union, 13

Berkeley Free Clinic, 171

Bernal Heights Community Corners Food Store. *See* Community Corners

bicycles and bicyclists, 98, 114, 172, 173

Bike Kitchen, 172

biodynamic agriculture, 69

BioFuel Oasis, 172

boards of directors, 76, 79, 87, 95, 112, 128, 134

bookkeeping, 65, 78, 88

Boston Mechanics' and Laborers' Mutual Benefit Association, 8

Bound Together Bookstore, 172

Box Dog Bikes, 172

boycotts, *18*, 21, 29, 39, 88; internal, 46, 59

BriarPatch Co-op (Grass Valley), 144n2, 150, 166

buildings, purchase of, 91, 93, 100n7, 115

bulk foods, 1, 2, 32, 54, 72, 104; Food Conspiracy, 25, 29, 105; Other Avenues, 83, 86, 88, 92, 97, 111; Rainbow, 76, 78, 80. *See also* warehouses; Yerba Buena Spice Collective

Burke, Angelynne, 95

business consultants. *See* consultants

business meetings, 37, 42, 65, 78–79, 85, 87, 88, 95; NoBAWC, 128

buying clubs. *See* food-buying clubs

California Center for Cooperative Development (CCCD), 55, 99, 129–30, 175

California Certified Organic Farmers (CCOF), 69, 169

California cuisine, 24, 54

California Food and Justice Coalition, 69

California Sustainable Agriculture, 114

Campbell, Lori, 35

Carson, Rachel: *Silent Spring*, 17

cashew chutney recipe, 119

Center for Urban Education, 69, 170

chain stores, 1, 30, 50, 71, 77, 81, 114, 122, 125

Chávez, César, 18, *18*, 19, 21

Cheese Board Collective, 86, 93, 112, 133–35

Cheese Board Pizzeria, 134, 172

chemical use in agriculture, 11, 12, 17, 21, 36

chilaquiles recipe, 27–28

child care, 23, 29, 43, 55, 108, 112. *See also* preschools

child-care centers, 32, 34, *41*

chutney, 109, 119

CoFed (Cooperative Food Empowerment Directive), 172

collective households, 55, 106–7

Collins, Joseph, 17, 138

communes, 24

Community Alliance with Family Farms, 169

Community Corners, 32, *41*

community food stores, 31–35 passim, 111. *See also* Haight Community Food Store; Inner Sunset Community Food Store; Noe Valley Community Store

community gardens, 52, 56, 114, 138, 143, *156*

community kitchens. *See* soup kitchens, community kitchens, etc.

community supported agriculture (CSA), 52, 130, 150, 169

conferences, 40, 130, 131

consensus decision making, 25–26, 32, 55, 63–67 passim, 85, 95, 141

construction projects, 75

consultants, 65, 88, 90, 112

Consumer Cooperative of Berkeley (CCB), 13–15, *13*, *22*, 34

# ABOUT THE AUTHOR

SHANTA NIMBARK SACHAROFF migrated from a small village in India to New York, eventually settling in San Francisco, where she felt at home with the foodcentric and co-op-friendly atmosphere. Shanta has been involved in the cooperative movement for more than three decades and works at Other Avenues, a worker-owned food co-op from the "new wave" co-op era of the 1970s. Shanta is a writer and contributes regularly to *India Currents*, an award-winning magazine. She also writes for various newsletters of the Bay Area's co-op organizations.

PM Press was founded at the end of 2007 by a small collection of folks with decades of publishing, media, and organizing experience. PM Press co-conspirators have published and distributed hundreds of books, pamphlets, CDs, and DVDs. Members of PM have founded enduring book fairs, spearheaded victorious tenant organizing campaigns, and worked closely with bookstores, academic conferences, and even rock bands to deliver political and challenging ideas to all walks of life. We're old enough to know what we're doing and young enough to know what's at stake.

We seek to create radical and stimulating fiction and non-fiction books, pamphlets, T-shirts, visual and audio materials to entertain, educate, and inspire you. We aim to distribute these through every available channel with every available technology—whether that means you are seeing anarchist classics at our bookfair stalls; reading our latest vegan cookbook at the café; downloading geeky fiction e-books; or digging new music and timely videos from our website.

PM Press is always on the lookout for talented and skilled volunteers, artists, activists, and writers to work with. If you have a great idea for a project or can contribute in some way, please get in touch.

PM Press
PO Box 23912
Oakland CA 94623
510-658-3906
www.pmpress.org

# FRIENDS OF PM

These are indisputably momentous times—the financial system is melting down globally and the Empire is stumbling. Now more than ever there is a vital need for radical ideas.

In the years since its founding—and on a mere shoestring—PM Press has risen to the formidable challenge of publishing and distributing knowledge and entertainment for the struggles ahead. With hundreds of releases to date, we have published an impressive and stimulating array of literature, art, music, politics, and culture. Using every available medium, we've succeeded in connecting those hungry for ideas and information to those putting them into practice.

Friends of PM allows you to directly help impact, amplify, and revitalize the discourse and actions of radical writers, filmmakers, and artists. It provides us with a stable foundation from which we can build upon our early successes and provides a much-needed subsidy for the materials that can't necessarily pay their own way. You can help make that happen—and receive every new title automatically delivered to your door once a month—by joining as a Friend of PM Press. And, we'll throw in a free T-shirt when you sign up.

Here are your options:
- $30 a month: Get all books and pamphlets plus 50% discount on all webstore purchases
- $40 a month: Get all PM Press releases (including CDs and DVDs) plus 50% discount on all webstore purchases
- $100 a month: Superstar—Everything plus PM merchandise, free downloads, and 50% discount on all webstore purchases

For those who can't afford $30 or more a month, we have Sustainer Rates at $15, $10, and $5. Sustainers get a free PM Press T-shirt and a 50% discount on all purchases from our website.

Your Visa or Mastercard will be billed once a month, until you tell us to stop. Or until our efforts succeed in bringing the revolution around. Or the financial meltdown of Capital makes plastic redundant. Whichever comes first.

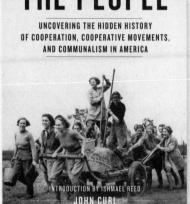

## For All the People
### Uncovering the Hidden History of Cooperation, Cooperative Movements, and Communalism in America, 2nd Edition

John Curl
Introduction by: Ishmael Reed

ISBN: 978-1-60486-582-0
9x6 • 608 Pages

Seeking to reclaim a history that has remained largely ignored by most historians, this dramatic and stirring account examines each of the definitive American cooperative movements for social change—farmer, union, consumer, and communalist—that have been all but erased from collective memory.

Focusing far beyond one particular era, organization, leader, or form of cooperation, *For All the People* documents the multigenerational struggle of the American working people for social justice. While the economic system was in its formative years, generation after generation of American working people challenged it by organizing visionary social movements aimed at liberating themselves from what they called wage slavery. Workers substituted a system based on cooperative work and constructed parallel institutions that would supersede the institutions of the wage system.

With an expansive sweep and breathtaking detail, this scholarly yet eminently readable chronicle follows the American worker from the colonial workshop to the modern mass-assembly line, from the family farm to the corporate hierarchy, ultimately painting a vivid panorama of those who built the United States and those who will shape its future.

John Curl, with over forty years of experience as both an active member and scholar of cooperatives, masterfully melds theory, practice, knowledge and analysis, to present the definitive history from below of cooperative America. This second edition contains a new introduction by Ishmael Reed; a new author's preface discussing cooperatives in the Great Recession of 2008 and their future in the 21st century; and a new chapter on the role co-ops played in the Food Revolution of the 1970s.